What Others A

One of the things I learned from my father, a long-time Texas Baptist pastor, was that when you take Christ out of the center, you begin to "wrangle" about peripheral things.

Terry Austin and Charlie Johnson are to be commended for their effort to beam the light of truth onto the crucial need for those of us who say we are followers of Christ to be conscious, intentional and passionate about returning Christ to the center. Pointing out how we in the church, the Body of Christ on earth, after all, have lost our way and ensnared ourselves in things out beyond concerns even with buildings and budgets, and issues that divide us from within and make us irrelevant and ineffective without.

I would love to be a member of Bread Fellowship, and I commend Terry, Charlie and the adventurers and pilgrims who have joined them on this exciting journey. God works mighty things through a remnant -- a group of people who remember just what it is we are about when we say that we are followers of Christ, attempting to be the church.

Read this book and name your own frustrations with what has happened to the church, carried off by thieves and robbers.

Read this book and call forth your inspirations for being a part of the remnant that wants to re-establish Jesus in his rightful place at the center -- of our personal lives and our life together.

Jeanie Miley
Author, "Joint Venture: Practical Spirituality for Everyday Pilgrims" and "Dance Lessons: Moving To the Beat of God's Heart"

The church in the West and especially here in America has become a country club. We have replaced unity with homogeneity, sameness. Everyone must look the same, act the same, believe exactly the same or they are made to feel unwelcome. This seems to be an extension of, or leads to the consumerist church. That place where one goes to have her needs and desires met. We go to be entertained, to meet likeminded people of our own socio-economic status, people just like us. While there is no dearth of books more than willing to point these ills out to us, Terry Austin in "Building a Church Without Fences" goes beyond and offers a model of how to overcome this trend. "Building a Church Without Fences" offers us insights on how to form authentic community out of which arises radical love. This book promotes radical inclusivity while telling us that it is the job of the Holy Spirit to change people, ours is to love them right where they are and provide a rich environment for the Spirit to do His work of transforming people into the image of Jesus. "Building a Church Without Fences" is a short, enjoyable read that packs a lot of insight into its just over 100 pages. I highly recommend this book.

Paul DeBaufer
Working in Christian recovery and one of those in the margins, unwanted in many churches, the despised, the unforgiven (by society and those in our churches) and one who stands with the disenfranchised and unwanted

I found much to think about in Terry's concise reflection on the church in the 21st century. Ours is a numbers culture, and that includes the church, which continues to measure success by the coins in the coffer or the people in the pews. Jesus affixed no numerical value to His command to love one another. He just said, "Go. Do this for me." Terry and Charlie are going and doing, led by the Holy Spirit to wherever it takes you. What freedom! What faith!

Jill "J.R." Labbe
Editorial Director, Fort Worth Star-Telegram

After reading the manuscript I became fascinated with the path Terry has taken, the journey he is on and what God has been teaching him. The illustrations he uses throughout his book come from his former experiences serving in the institutional church and his present experiences exploring a more organic form of church (Bread Fellowship). I found his illustrations brought back memories of times spent serving as a professional minister and similar stories shared with me by many of my friends. This made it easy for me to relate to the gist of his book. There were numerous times I found myself experiencing uh-huh moments as Terry shared from his many years of ministry and life experience.

The journey God is leading Terry on appears to be very similar to the one God has been leading me and many of my friends on over the past number of years. I look forward to discovering, alongside Terry, the destination Jesus has in mind for those wanting to remove the barriers that continually keep us from sharing the truth with everyone who wants to hear it. "Acceptance, Forgiveness, and Love: Building a Church without Fences" is a book that will provide a great deal of food for thought on how we need to listen to Jesus, be obedient to Him and teach others by example (be accepting, be forgiving and be loving) to do the same.

Rob Ross
Disciple of Jesus, Facilitator for Oikos Ministries, husband, father, friend, online missionary, writer, storyteller, and chaplain

ACCEPTANCE, FORGIVENESS, AND LOVE:

BUILDING A CHURCH WITHOUT FENCES

TERRY AUSTIN

Acceptance, Forgiveness, and Love: Building a
Church without Fences

Published by Austin Brothers Publishing

Keller, Texas

www.austinbrotherspublishing.com

ISBN 978-0-9853263-2-6

Austin Brothers
Publishing

Printed in the United States of America

2012 -- First Edition

To all the amazing people of
Bread Fellowship.

An eclectic group of
followers of Christ
striving to relate to others with
acceptance, forgiveness, and love.

CONTENTS

FOREWORD

Alfred Loisy, a great Roman Catholic New Testament scholar, once said, "Jesus preached the Kingdom of God, and the Church was the result." He meant that Jesus didn't envision a vast hierarchical structure spread throughout the world. None of us can say what he intended with reference to church. From his disciples to our own day we who believe have tried to figure out how best to bring to expression in our times and circumstances what he, still living among us, wants. Bread Fellowship, founded in Fort Worth, Texas, by Charlie Johnson and Terry Austin is one of the most remarkable creative efforts to do what Jesus wanted that I have seen or studied in church history.

Bread Fellowship is clearly an alternative way of being church. They have no aspirations to become a mega-church or even what sociologist Wade Clark Roof has called meta-church, a church with traditional structures. Rather, they center everything on Jesus and decline to delineate a circumference. They are a church without walls, inclusive rather than exclusive. Such an approach, of course, suggests that they, like the Apostle Paul, have confidence that God, the Living Christ, will do something we humans can't do, namely, transform lives. Although both Johnson and Austin have experienced successful ministries in large traditional congregations, they here serve in modest ways as facilitators of this fellowship, whose center is Jesus Christ.

"Bread" reminds me of the meals Jesus met with his disciples to eat. The "last" supper was not the only meal they ate together. Breaking bread together facilitated fellowship. Notice in the Gospels how often Jesus ate with people; that bonded him to them. And I think that must happen in Bread Fellowship, where they meet on Sunday evenings and, as a rule, observe the Lord's Supper together. It happens that this kind of approach is reaching a group of people somewhat turned off by churches that define themselves in terms of circumference rather than by the center, Jesus.

A very important element in the modus operandi of Bread Fellowship is hospitality. Like Jesus himself, it is non-judgmental. Censoriousness all too easily creeps into church life, just as it pervades our whole culture. The consequence is partisanship and bitter battles, both public and private. But here is a church in which the keynote is: "You are accepted." Bread Fellowship sounds amazingly like early Christian communities before very much organization took over and people started clamoring to run things according to their rules.

What about the future of a creative community like this? It won't supplant mega-churches, meta-churches, and a vast array of other church organizations and institutions in America any more than early Christian "house churches" displaced the state cultus or the oriental religions in the Roman Empire. All of them continued for centuries. But Bread Fellowship is discharging a mission in Fort Worth the other churches aren't and can't do. It functions much like those early Christian communities that met in homes or wherever they could find a place, even in the catacombs under the city. So long as they keep Christ at the center and fellowship with him and with one another as the focus, they will have something to offer the world, the world doesn't already have more of than it needs.

By the way, this is an engaging and readable book. You will find not only a good picture of Bread Fellowship but also an open and honest introduction to Terry Austin. I have not met Terry personally, but I feel after reading his book that I know him. I have known Charlie Johnson from many years ago when he took classes and came often to talk in my office at Southern Seminary. I vouch for anything he undertakes in ministry.

E. Glenn Hinson
Professor of Church History and Spirituality
Baptist Seminary of Kentucky
Baptist Theological Seminary at Richmond (retired)
Southern Baptist Theological Seminary (retired)

INTRODUCTION

In Kuala Lumpur, Malaysia, it is easy to spot the Petronas Towers. These twin towers were the tallest buildings in the world from 1994 until 2008. They still remain as the tallest twin towers in the world. Building skyscrapers is an amazing process that requires a tremendous amount of planning and knowledge. One of the most unique features of the Petronas Towers is the foundation of the buildings. At 394 feet, the towers hold claim to the deepest foundation in the world. It took twelve months and massive amounts of concrete and steel to build the foundation.

Every contractor, in fact, every child who has ever tried to stack dominoes or blocks, understands the necessity of a good foundation. The reason for the extreme size of this foundation is because of the depth of the bedrock in Malaysia. Even forty stories worth of concrete must sit on something solid in order to support a structure. Without good support, every structure will eventually topple.

Understanding the need for a good foundation raises a red flag as I think about the modern church in America. Before explaining my concern, I probably need to make a short statement of what I see happening in the church today. The majority of churches can be fit into two categories. (Don't you love people who can classify everything into two categories?)

The first category is those churches that are consumer driven and entertainment focused. Plans are made and programs implemented on the basis of what people outside the church want. The rationale is when the church offers what people want, they will come. These offerings include music style, recreation opportunities, children's activities, and family events. This is why I say these churches are also entertainment focused. Great emphasis is placed on high quality because of the belief people expect their entertainment to be good and must compete with what they can find in the secular world.

Let me be quick to ask you not to misunderstand what I am saying. In defining these churches as consumer driven and entertainment focused I am not being critical. Their intention is good. They are striving to attract people so they will hear and respond to the Gospel. Many of these churches are very effective and gather enormous crowds who are then provided with a powerful presentation of the Christian message (although the message might get swallowed up in the method). Tremendous amounts of time, effort, and money are expended week after week in order to bring people to the church.

Many churches in this first category have grown to be extremely large, which in turn has caused many others to follow their lead. The pressing need is for church leaders who are charismatic (in personality, not necessarily theologically), driven, good communicators (verbally and/or musically), and attractive.

This category of churches contains most of the very fast growing churches in our country. These congregations are attracting large groups of people, most of them from the second category of churches that I will define shortly. These churches are constructing a massive structure and make a huge mark on the religious landscape of our world.

The second major category of churches in this country can be described as tradition bound and struggling for survival. These churches continue to do church just like they have for the past few generations. Many of these churches have a rich history of service and success and a few of them are still doing an effective job of reaching people and experiencing growth.

For these churches, the goal is to preserve approaches and methods that have proven successful in the past. Tradition and maintaining ties to the historic faith are important. They are typically very tenacious about who they are and what they believe. The vast majority of these churches are members of mainline Christian denominations that are all experiencing decline. In fact, most of these churches are also declining in attendance and participation.

It is not uncommon to find these churches trying to maintain large buildings that are in need of expensive repairs. It might be a church with four hundred people meeting in a sanctuary that once housed a thousand or a congregation of forty trying to maintain a building that was constructed for two hundred. These churches are common in rural communities, but are also quite prevalent in the city.

One thing that churches in both categories have in common is that they are locked into a situation where they must maintain a massive structure with a very small, inadequate foundation. The consumer driven and entertainment focused church probably has a large building to maintain, but they also have put themselves in the position of providing expensive programs that require lavish equipment. This structure often rests on a foundation of believers who do not have much of a history of church support or those who come just for the experience.

When you look at the numerous studies that have been done about the church today, you will understand my concern that we are resting on a very inadequate foundation. It has been estimated that churches are spending more than ninety percent of their income on themselves. In addition to this concern, is the fact that even among those who are regular attendees, there is an abundance of ignorance about the Christian faith. Decades of topical problem-solving preaching has produced congregations that leave their Bibles at home on Sunday; many don't even read them during the week.

My concern is that the church cannot continue to support this structure with an uneducated, self-seeking congregation. We have expended enormous resources building a great looking church but we have neglected to provide the necessary foundation. The necessary foundation is made up of deep faith, prolific knowledge of the faith, and generosity toward others. Much of it is lacking in today's church.

When a church is built on the idea that bigger and glitzier is better, it develops a voracious appetite for money. It is expensive to keep providing bigger and glitzier. If we had a music evangelist last year, this year we must have a contemporary recording artist, and next year we must find a Christian pop star to share a testimony. If we don't, the mega church down the highway will and folks will flock over there.

The result is enormous buildings that require maintenance, large staffs that need good salaries, and high utility bills. Even more importantly, the real need is for mature leadership. However, when the church has invested all of its resources in attracting new people, little has been done in the way of discipleship and leadership development.

That is why I am concerned that today's church might collapse. It seems that we have built a skyscraper by taking all the little pieces and stacking them together without developing the necessary foundation. It can only go so far before it begins to crumble. We are gathering people from smaller churches where they provided leadership and stability, packing them together in an auditorium, and think we are building the church. However, now that they are in an enormous congregation, all they really need to do is sit and enjoy (or perhaps help park cars once a month).

It is time to roll up our sleeves and start digging in order to repair the foundation!

Growing up and being educated and trained as a Southern Baptist, I have worshipped around the altar of church growth. Everything is about increasing the size of the church, getting more people to "join the church" and come to the Sunday morning services. I have been a pastor and felt the pressure of reporting good attendance week after week. Many ministry failures can be excused as long as the average attendance increases year after year.

As a child, I was encouraged to memorize "The Great Commission" at the end of Matthew's Gospel where Jesus instructed his followers to go out and grow the church. If there was ever a concern about focusing too much on numbers we were told that it is biblical – the Book of Acts records three thousand being saved in one day and there is an entire book of the Old Testament with the name Numbers.

When I was the pastor of a very rural church with virtually no possibility of increased membership numbers, I struggled with thinking I was doing something wrong. Perhaps I was not working hard enough or maybe I simply was not the pastor this community needed. Back in those days, the Southern Baptist Convention gave an award to the "Small Church Pastor of the Year." However, it was always given to a pastor who had turned a small church into a large church.

It now seems that some folks have figured out how to do this and they are growing churches into the thousands and ten thousands. In the Dallas/Fort Worth Metroplex where I live there are numerous churches that have more than a thousand attend every week. They can be found in every nook and cranny of the city. Perhaps a half a dozen or more of these churches report more than ten thousand in attendance. Church growth has been a success!

Or has it?

I have studied the New Testament for many years and have come to the conclusion that the work of the church is not about enormous growth. Especially when you study the ministry of Jesus, there is little concern about accumulating large numbers of followers. In fact, it sounds like Jesus almost made it impossible for large numbers of people to follow him. Listen to these verses:

"Enter through the narrow gate; for the gate is wide and the way is broad that leads to destruction, and there are many who enter through it. For the gate is small and the way is narrow that leads to life, and there are few who find it." (Matthew 7:13-14)

"And he who does not take his cross and follow after Me is not worthy of Me. He who has found his life will lose it, and he who has lost his life for My sake will find it." (Matthew 10:38-39)

Then Jesus said to His disciples, "If anyone wishes to come after Me, he must deny himself, and take up his cross and follow Me. For whoever wishes to save his life will lose it; but whoever loses his life for My sake will find it." (Matthew 16:24-25)

These verses are just a sample of many of the things Jesus did that would discourage and drive away a crowd.

Perhaps these words of Jesus suggest that those who have been successful at growing a large congregation might have done so at the cost of changing the message. There is simply no mass appeal in these words. I'm not saying that God cannot or will not bring together a large group of people. It happened in the book of Acts and it has happened a few times in history since. However, it is certainly not the norm and I would not expect to find hundreds of these unusual congregations in north Texas.

There is an interesting testimony about this matter in Christianity Today. Walter Kallestad was pastor of a two hundred member church in Phoenix. While standing in line to purchase tickets for a movie he had an epiphany. "The only way to capture people's attention is entertainment, I thought. If I want people to listen to my message, I've got to present it in a way that grabs their attention long enough for me to communicate the gospel."

Not surprisingly, it worked. "For us, worship was a show, and we played to a packed house. We grew by thousands, bought more land, and positioned ourselves to reach even more people. Not that any of this is wrong in and of itself - people coming to faith in Christ isn't bad. I told myself it was good - I told others it was good... By the time we service the $12-million debt, pay the staff, and maintain the property, we've spent more than a million before we can spend a dime on our mission. At the time, we had plans for a spectacular worship center with a retractable roof."

After some serious soul searching, time in prayer, and study of what God was doing with other congregations, Kallestad came to this conclusion: "We were entertaining people as a substitute for leading them into the presence of God."

This church made an immediate change from entertainment to learning how to enter into true worship of God and relationships with one another. People responded in the same way they responded to Jesus – they left. However, as the church changed something even more significant happened. "I used to ask, 'What can we do to get more people to attend our church?' Now I ask, 'How can I best equip and empower the people to go be the church in the marketplace where God has called them to serve?'"

This is real church growth. Not necessarily numerical growth but growth toward becoming more like Jesus. It will probably never be an especially popular type of increase because it cannot be measured so we cannot take credit for it. Jesus' message is hard. Although His miraculous works attracted large crowds, his message scattered them quickly.

I think true church growth should be less about attracting large crowds to come and "be blessed" by our great music, awesome programs, and attractive facilities and more about sending followers of Jesus into the world to bless others. It is time to move away from the model of growth that we have adopted from the business world and return to a model of growth that focuses on spiritual depth and relationship.

If this idea catches on there might still be hope for me to win that award for Small Church Pastor of the Year.

One of the reasons I struggle with my feelings about the church is because the reality I see all around me seems to be in contrast to the promise made by Jesus.

And Jesus said to him, "Blessed are you, Simon Barjona, because flesh and blood did not reveal this to you, but My Father who is in heaven. I also say to you that you are Peter, and upon this rock I will build My church; and the gates of Hades will not overpower it."
(Matthew 16:17-18)

The key phrase of this statement is that "the gates of Hades will not overpower it (the church)." Nothing, not even the power of death and hell can stand in the way of the church. Jesus assures His followers that the church will overcome all foes and obstacles and achieve its proper purpose.

It is tempting to relegate this to some future promise when we expect, in the end, the church will be the only thing left standing. But, Jesus' promise seems to have present implications. The church should be able to march against all enemies and come away victorious. All goals should be achieved, all needs met, and all battles won. Not even Satan himself is powerful enough to stop the church.

There is something wrong with the way we are doing church. It has taken sixty years of life and thirty-five years of ministry for me to realize it, but I have an idea of what is going on. That is the reason for this book.

Genesis

I met Charlie when he was the interim pastor of the church Sharon and I attended. It's hard to say why we were attending that particular church. It's a very liturgical congregation, something I have always appreciated but high church ritual doesn't do much for Sharon. We ended up there because we had tried every other style of church in the city and always ended up disappointed or worse.

Our journey toward finding the right church for us has taken many winding paths. When I left my job as pastor, more than two decades ago, I took a position working as a church consultant. Consequently, I travelled a bunch and visited every kind of church imaginable. As a consultant, I got involved with church leadership, listened to their vision and dreams, participated in their activities, and came to appreciate a wide variety of church styles.

Although it is true that every church is different, I discovered the Christian landscape consists of churches with a great deal in common. There are primarily older churches that have to look to the past to see their better days. These churches are trying to hold on to something that is of little interest to most people today. They are located in inner cities and country settings. There is little hope they will survive because to survive they would have to change and change is the one thing they dread the most.

The other style of doing church is much livelier, filled with younger crowds, often meeting in state-of-the-art facilities, and characterized by energetic music and presentations. Although it is fun to attend these churches, whenever I left it felt like I had been to a show rather than church. My wife actually attended one where the pastor was preaching a series with a superhero theme (I'm not sure what the point was) and on that particular Sunday they did a Batman reenactment, complete with fighting on stage. It was like attending Community Theater.

Neither of these styles of church provided what I felt church should be, but we had settled with one in the looking to the past category and that's where we were when we met Charlie. Every Sunday morning it felt like we were really going to church as we passed through the thick wooden doors in the front of a massive, gothic type structure with beautiful stained glass windows. I have never been a fan of attending church in a building that looks like a big box department store on the outside and a sterile community theater on the inside and this place really felt like being at church.

We liked the church but it always felt like something was missing. Our Sunday School class was good, people were friendly, music was great. We even managed to make the Wednesday evening meal upon occasion and attended a couple of business meetings (the true sign of a committed church member). Because of my background and experience, I was asked to serve on the Endowment Committee, a place where it was obvious after one or two meetings that I did not fit. Sharon enjoyed helping a group of young Korean women learn English, but as hard as we tried, we never felt like we belonged.

When Charlie became our pastor we did not anticipate much to change in our relationship with the church. I had actually met him many years earlier but I'm sure he does not remember. I'm not even sure why I remember. It was in the parking garage of the office building of Texas Baptists where I worked. We met at the elevator. I guarantee you cannot ride an elevator with Charlie, even for one or two floors, without having a new friend. I knew who he was, the pastor of a large church in San Antonio, but he had no reason to know anything about me. At the church in Fort Worth, we became friends.

Charlie invited us to attend a Thursday morning Bible study he led every week and we did. We enjoyed the group but he kept telling us we might like an evening study he was leading even better. As you might imagine, the morning group consisted of folks who were free during the day so the average age was much older than us. Although I am in a wheelchair, I was probably the healthiest man in the group. We did attend the evening group and felt more at home with the younger crowd, although we were now the "old folks."

Our church called a full time pastor and Charlie moved on to other things, but we continued with the Bible study groups. During that time we had numerous conversations about the church and what we should be doing. Charlie kept telling me that some of the folks in his Bible study groups were interested in having a time of worship.

Our friendship with Charlie strengthened significantly when I was in the hospital in critical condition immediately after Christmas in 2009. He came to the

Intensive Care unit and led in prayer – a prayer that I am confident God used to impact my life. I sometimes say that I credit Charlie with saving my life and I am not kidding.

Both of us felt a burden to do something different. We had been listening to the young people in the evening Bible study group. They had an interest in spiritual matters but very little interest in the church. This was difficult to understand for those of us who had spent our entire lives actively involved with church.

Charlie came to our house and had a prayer time with Sharon and me. During the visit it seemed as if God confirmed something in the heart of all of us. We thought it was time to start a worship service, building from the members of the Bible study groups. We chose Sunday evenings for a couple of reasons. Charlie was still preaching frequently on Sunday mornings and he wanted to continue to be available. Perhaps more important was that it seemed like a better time for those we wanted to be involved in the worship time. It was too much to expect young people who are not currently involved in church to get up early on Sunday morning.

In the fall of 2009 we held our first worship service. Meeting in the community room of the apartment complex where Charlie lived, the place was full. The majority of attendees on that first Sunday were folks who wanted to support our efforts but who had little interest in being a part of a new church. They quickly faded away and we had to begin building from scratch. Today, there are very few remnants of that first service.

We call our little congregation Bread Fellowship. We have a very simple, yet clear mission statement – "Eat.

Feed." We gather to eat, both spiritually and often physically, then we scatter to feed others, again both spiritually and physically.

In one of our early times together, Charlie made a statement that has stuck with me and has really become a theme of what we are trying to do together. Quoting something he had heard, he said, "The church should have Christ as the center and no circumference."

We have heard time and again that an enormous number of people have great respect for Jesus but want nothing to do with the church. In other words, they like the center (Jesus) but they don't want anything to do with where we draw the circumference line – the line that determines who is in and who is out, who is right and who is wrong. The reason they feel this way is because we tend to spend most of our time focusing on the circumference and not so much time on the center.

I have been actively engaged with the church all my life. I have been a pastor and a church consultant my entire adult life. Having preached in as many as five hundred churches, I have some definite opinions about how we do church. I realize that I am generalizing, but I have come to believe there are only four different ways to draw the circumference line. Each would fight you if you suggest that anything other than Christ is at the center. However, it is the circumference where they differ:

- Fundamentalist – They have a very small circle (not number of folks, but acceptable beliefs and activities) with a clear, impenetrable line for their circumference.

- Conservative – They move the circumference line out a little and it might not be quite so clear, but it is still there. They might not kick you out if you cross the line but they will certainly let you know when you are in error.

- Moderate – Once again they move the circumference line a little farther out, being more acceptable of certain behaviors and beliefs. These folks are actually willing to allow people in leadership positions who would not even be allowed to belong to a fundamentalist congregation.

- Liberal – They often get accused of not having any rules or limits but they do. In fact, they spend a great deal of time and energy debating that it is acceptable to believe and do things that many other churches consider ungodly and disgusting.

The one thing each of the groups have in common is that they have a circumference – a line drawn that determines who does and does not belong. The reason so many are not interested in these churches is because they spend a great deal of effort fighting over where to draw the line. These skirmishes are what drive people away from the church, in spite of the fact they are attracted to Jesus.

Thus, at Bread Fellowship, we have determined to focus our attention on Christ and leave the circumference up to Him. Consequently, everyone is welcome. We like to say that we are a faith community with Christ at the center and where everyone is welcome. This does not mean that anything goes when we gather for worship. We strive to worship Christ and our understanding of Him is guided by God's Word.

However, rather than determining who is or is not a believer, we try to just point to Christ and allow Him to do the judging. Our focus is on the center, not the circumference. Obviously, this opens us up to criticism, especially from the circumference police, but I am convinced if we can continually point people to Jesus, He will do the job of getting their lives correct.

Everyone is welcome at Bread – believer, unbeliever, agnostic, or whatever else you consider yourself. When you come you will be invited to join a discussion of a text from God's Word, your opinion will be welcome. It is unlikely that anyone will say you are incorrect or worthy of damnation, instead we will try to point you once again to Christ. All you will be expected to do is respect our beliefs and opinions, as we will respect yours, and we encourage you to give them some thought. If you have a need, we will pray for you and we would love to have you pray for us, even if you pray in an unorthodox manner.

Almost every church advertises that everyone is welcome, often accompanied with the phrase, "come as you are." While it is true that everyone is invited and likely that no one will be turned away for who they are or how they appear, that does not necessarily mean they are welcome. What it often means is you are welcome to come but as soon as you get here we expect you to become like us. If you have a drinking or drug problem people will keep their distance. If you had an abortion they will probably make you feel like a murderer. If you happen to be Democrat they will make you feel like an idiot.

What we strive to do at Bread Fellowship is to welcome you in without asking you to change. Our hope is that you will participate in our worship and respond to our fellowship so that you will be drawn toward the center – Christ. When that occurs, He will do the changing. This creates some messy situations at times and it means we have a very eclectic group in our fellowship.

Our goal is not to change people. Our task is to lift up Jesus (Christ in the center). We have deliberately chosen not to build professional quality worship experiences or obtain a state-of-the-art facility. Instead, we see ourselves as a group of believers who gather around Christ. The gatherings happen in homes, parks, community rooms, and churches – wherever we can find the space. We sing, we pray, we study God's Word, we fellowship, we encourage, and we almost always share Communion together.

We talk and pray a great deal about the direction of Bread Fellowship. Several amazing things have happened. Everyone who participates is there because of a relationship with someone in our group, they were brought by someone. I think this is great because it shows our evangelism is happening outside of our worship time. It also makes it easier to incorporate them into the body because they already have a connection. We have only had two people show up out of the clear blue and we have had a difficult time establishing a continuing relationship with them.

Bread Fellowship has become the product of all our individuals coming together. We are who we are together. We have not set out to become anything in particular. The music we sing, the discussions we have, the fellowship we share are not preplanned to be a certain way, they are a reflection of us. Every person who joins our group changes the makeup of the group.

Charlie and I might be more vocal than most of the others but we are aware that we are no more important. God is putting together a very unique group that we call Bread Fellowship and we are honored to belong.

The downside is that numerical growth is slow (if that is really a downside). We could plan some big events; Charlie is a marvelous communicator with much experience speaking to large crowds. But, we have chosen not to do that. Instead of attracting a crowd, we are trying to build a church. One person at a time, we are inviting family, friends, co-workers, and other acquaintances to come. They will feel welcomed, everyone does. We will ask about them, talk to them, allow them to share in everything, and at the very least they will be drawn closer to Jesus. The closer they get to Christ, the less important is the baggage they bring with them.

When we say, "Come as you are, all are welcome," we really mean it. We will not try to change you, guilt you, condemn you, or criticize you. We will simply invite you to journey through life with us and see what happens.

We are truly trying to work out the concept of Christ at the center without a circumference. It might be there is a model here for how to do church. It is not news that young people are leaving the church. They remain interested in spiritual matters but they are not finding what they need at church. I am convinced the predominate model for doing church today – the megachurch – will not endure much longer. It is too cumbersome, too dependent upon high profile personalities, and too high maintenance. Besides the fact many are leaving after the Sunday morning service, like I often did, still feeling that something is missing, even after the good show.

This book is about building a church without a circumference. I am aware that I am working without a net and many of you (probably some that I consider friends) will disagree and think I have jumped the shark. To be honest, this concept of doing church has been formulating in my mind for a long time. Charlie and I will be the first to admit that we had no idea of what we were doing when we started on this journey together. We were simply striving to follow the leadership of God's Spirit. That is not to blame God for what we have done but simply to indicate that we are doing our best to figure it out as we go.

I am also confident that we are not at the place on the journey to be writing a book about how to do what we did. Consequently, this will be more like a journal describing the trip than a how-to book. Almost every week I am amazed at what God is doing in our community. I am also aware that at any moment, God might take us off in another direction that we have not anticipated, such is the nature of the Christian life.

But, I think it is possible to have a church with Christ at the center and no circumference. If you have any interest in that concept, I invite you to join me on the journey to see where we end up. There is still much to do and much to learn.

THE HUMAN HISTORY OF BUILDING FENCES

There are really only two things you need to know about Luigi – he lived in a small seaside village and he was a painter. Not a house painter but an artist. He spent many days sitting on the hill outside his cottage, gazing into the ocean, and painting what he saw. One day it all came together for Luigi and he painted the most amazing landscape ever seen.

Being proud of his work, Luigi hung the painting in the front room of his small house and invited his neighbors to come view his work. They did and they were amazed. The picture looked as real as if they were gazing out the back window toward the real ocean. They couldn't keep quiet and kept inviting friends to see the amazing painting. It was apparent that Luigi could not keep the painting in his small front room so he wrapped it up and carried it into town to the local museum.

The curator was not interested in Luigi at first, but once the painting was unwrapped, he immediately grabbed it and hung it in the prime spot in the museum. Soon there were long lines of people waiting to see the painting. But there was a problem. The painting was so real that people were tempted to touch it just to make sure they weren't looking out a window or that the water wasn't real.

The curator couldn't have people touching the artwork so he positioned a small fence to keep people back. Yet the attraction was so great that many would stretch across the fence and touch it just to make sure. So he moved the fence back a few feet but still folks would climb on top of the fence and stretch just to touch. The curator had to build a taller fence and eventually he put a clear Plexiglas shield in front of the painting. Eventually he even put a cover over the top to make sure people wouldn't try to throw a coin or something else into the picture of the ocean.

Now people could not actually see the painting so the curator printed brochures that described the painting and provided it for the people to read as they stood in line. The painting was just as beautiful as ever and people came to the museum from all over the land but all they ever saw was a nice brochure and a good fence.

I like fences. Since I grew up having to walk on crutches, balance has always been a primary concern for me. A good fence often serves as protection, to keep me from falling off a ledge or stepping into something I should avoid. I always loved handrails on stairs, which are very similar to fences. They provide protection and security.

Several years ago our family visited one of those big caverns that tourists like to tour. We went to the bottom of the cave, taking my wheelchair all the way down. We were then told it was necessary to climb about forty-five narrow stairs in order to exit the cave. We looked for other options but there were none (a rather long story not necessary for my purposes here). My brother had to pick me up and carry me up the stairs, holding me out over the railing in order to maneuver the narrow stairs.

I trust my brother completely and I have full confidence in his physical ability to carry me – he is a large guy. However, I must confess it was rather stressful since the fence that was designed to keep folks from falling off the stairs would have done me no good if he had slipped. Imagine standing on the edge a fifth floor balcony without a fence. I do like fences.

All of us appreciate fences. In fact, humans have been building fences for a long time. Fences keep us safe and provide a feeling of security, allowing us to hold certain things in and providing a barrier to hold other things out.

Religious fences are also important. When I first became serious about being a student of the Bible, I learned the Pharisees of Jesus' day were excellent fence builders. Every Bible teacher worthy of the title taught the concept of Pharisees using their plethora of laws as a means of building a fence around God's law. It was their way of protecting themselves from being disobedient.

Perhaps the clearest expression of this kind of religious fence building was the way they handled rules about the Sabbath. The Sabbath was established by God and made His list of top ten (see Exodus twenty). However, the problem with God's law-giving is that He was seldom specific enough for us. Ok, so I want to keep the Sabbath holy but what does that mean? How do I do that? What should I do on the Sabbath? What should I not do on the Sabbath? These are all important questions.

Since God wasn't talking, the Pharisees decided to specify what could and could not be done, just to make sure that everyone was safe. They calculated how much distance a person could walk before the Sabbath became unholy. They also specified how much weight you could carry, what kind of work you could do, everything down to the minutest detail. They had hundreds (some have suggested thousands) of laws designed to protect the holiness of the Sabbath.

Like Luigi's painting, the Sabbath actually disappeared from sight. It no longer mattered. All that concerned the Pharisees was maintaining the fence. By the way, they did this with all of God's laws, making all of them inaccessible. Jesus came along and turned their world upside down by suggesting God wasn't interested in their fences.

I understand why the Pharisees did what they did. Have I mentioned that I like fences? It is comforting to know that if I do certain things and avoid other things God will be pleased. Just tell me what to do and I will do it. Even if I lean up against the fence, or God forbid, climb over the fence on occasion, at least it keeps me far enough away that I won't be doing anything offensive to God.

Although the Pharisees were excellent fence builders, the practice did not stop when they disappeared from the scene. Church folks have been building fences ever since.

It is often said that people like Jesus but they don't want anything to do with the church. I think what that means is they like Jesus but they don't like the fences that we have built around Him. We have built numerous fences, for several reasons. First, we want to make sure the right people get in. We want churches that have people just like us, or at least people who want to be just like us. That is why affinity churches are so popular.

One of the latest fads is cowboy churches. I attended one a while back and the entire sermon was on how to bridle a horse for the best control. They frequently (perhaps every Sunday afternoon) gather for a roping in a rodeo arena after church. You are most comfortable wearing jeans and cowboy boots. Sure, they talk about Jesus, but perhaps the best thing their fences do is to make sure they get the right people in.

Just as important to fence builders is to keep the wrong people out. If you don't want anyone who likes to have a glass of wine or an occasional beer, build a fence and simply declare that real followers of Jesus don't drink. Fences come in a variety of shapes and styles. If you don't want to associate with Democrats, just adopt the Republican platform as something blessed by Jesus. Certainly you don't want your children influenced by gays so build a fence that keeps them out.

Churches have built fences to keep people out based on lifestyle, belief, ethnicity, politics, race, and past sins. Virtually anything that you can use to classify a person can be, and has been, used as a fence to keep people away from Jesus. We want church to be comfortable so we find ways to keep out the people who make us uncomfortable. Our preference is that others find a church of their own kind. For example, the homeless should attend a church for the homeless but don't stain our pews with your unwashed clothes and body odor.

Sometimes, the ones who most like fences are parents of young children. They want a safe environment that will pass on their faith to their children. So they gather in churches that offer colorful facilities, screened workers, and quality programs and activities. The more activities that keep their children busy and occupied the better. In fact, if the church offers all our children's recreational, educational, social, and entertainment needs, that is ideal. There is no need to expose them to many other potentially dangerous influences.

I must hasten to add churches don't blatantly advertise these fences. It is much more subtle. Say a young person comes to church one Sunday morning, hair spiked straight up and arms covered with colorful tattoos. The usher might actually speak a word of greeting and hand him a worship folder. But the fences immediately go up as people stare, point, and whisper to one another. Most of us are very adept at communicating our disfavor and unacceptance of another without actually saying anything.

At other times we are very vocal about our fences. Christians in the media speak of inappropriate lifestyles and condemn folks who don't live up to our standards. It has taken years but the church has effectively communicated that certain people don't belong in our churches. These people know they are not welcome because they are on the wrong side of the fence. They are tired of being criticized, belittled, and ostracized. Consequently, they want nothing to do with the church, in spite of the fact that they like what they hear about Jesus.

A couple of years ago I met a very nice man in a hospital waiting room and we had time for an extended conversation. He talked for a long time about politics, being very clear about his desire to elect a new President and his confidence that if we will simply choose a few more Republicans all of our problems will be solved. I didn't offer much of an opinion since it was clear that his beliefs were much more important to him than mine were to me. I listened patiently.

He then turned the conversation to his church. He spoke graciously about his church and pastor and suggested that I would like it. He even invited me to attend in the near future. I'm sorry, but I could not resist the temptation to ask if it was necessary to be a Republican in order to come to his church. I even asked if they had a separate Sunday School class for Democrats.

My new friend was stunned for a moment, almost as if I had kicked his dog. We had a short conversation about making people comfortable or turning them away by our overly strong political opinions. Someone who favors the Republican platform would probably be very welcome; however, many young people are turned away, not because they are rejecting the Gospel but because they are rejecting the politics.

I have not attended his church so I don't know for sure, but I suspect that anyone not favorable toward Republican politics would soon feel like they were on the outside of the fence. It might be things said in the sermon or during a Sunday School class. Perhaps it is simply the hallway banter or overheard conversations in the foyer. It is easy to erect fences that keep people away while at the same time advertising that everyone is welcome.

The problem is that we have built so many fences over the years that nearly everyone who does not conform to a specific way of life feels like they do not belong. The more secular our world becomes, the higher we build the fences. It is tempting to circle the wagons even tighter in order to protect ourselves, our children, and our stuff.

A few years ago my next door neighbor's house was burglarized during the day. The thieves went through his gate, broke in the back door, opened the garage and backed their van in and loaded it up. They stole some electronics and a few miscellaneous items, even a pizza from the freezer. My neighbor's response was to get a new alarm system and build a bigger fence around his back yard. He tore down the builder quality fence that matched everyone else in the neighborhood and replaced it with a much taller fence and better wood. He even attached an expensive lock on the gate.

Robert Frost told us that good fences make good neighbors. However, they do not make good friends. Neither do they make for good churches.

THE ATTRACTING POWER OF CHRIST

Tallahassee, Florida is the location of the world's largest manmade magnet. Twenty-two feet tall and weighing thirty-four tons, it has the magnetic force equivalent to one million times the pull of earth's gravity. You probably don't want to be in the same room with your car keys in your front pocket.

The church has tried just about everything, except the powerful Tallahassee magnet, to attract people. I get one or two pieces of mail every week inviting me to a particular church in my neighborhood. Big electronic signs and massive billboards can be seen from the Interstate near my house, all designed to attract me to a church. (Come to think about it, churches are spending great amounts of money to invite me to attend but seldom have I been personally invited to church.)

Churches seem to be convinced the key to success is to attract as many people as possible. About twenty years ago, one of the funniest things I have ever heard about happened to my father. To understand this event you have to know that my father had an artificial leg, having lost his right leg during the Big War in the Pacific. This loss occurred before I was born so I didn't know him when he had both legs. Having what we always called a "wooden leg" was no big deal for any of us, although they quit making them out of wood a long time ago.

Daddy always liked to have fun with his circumstances and he would often pretend to be knocking on some little kid's head while simultaneously rapping on his leg, making it sound like they had a wooden head. At night he would stand his leg in the corner of the bathroom, which occasionally freaked out some folks when we had friends spend the night. Daddy knew how to make the best out of a tough situation.

The incident I remember so vividly occurred in the foyer at City Hall in Amarillo, Texas. He and my mother had just moved into town and he went to get the utilities turned on at their new house. It was a rainy day, an unusual thing in the Texas panhandle. Any kind of precipitation always made walking with a wooden leg a little treacherous. If you have ever tried to walk without steady support, you know that two of the worst enemies are ice and wet tile.

As he stepped into the foyer, his right leg, the artificial one, slipped out from under him and down he went. I'm sure it was an event worthy of a YouTube moment. Daddy was uninjured but he had a serious problem. As a result of the fall, his wooden leg came loose from his stump. Now he had a conundrum. His leg was dangling in his pants and he couldn't put it back on nor could he slide it out of his pants. Remember, the upper part of your leg will not fit through your pant leg.

His leg was held on by creating suction to his stump. This was accomplished by using a stocking. Daddy had a stocking in the glove compartment of his car so he had one of several helpful observers retrieve it for him. However, in order to put his leg back on, he had to drop his pants. If you have ever been in a difficult situation, you have discovered that people want to help. Such was the case. A group of men gathered around him, blocking him from view, while he slid his pants to the floor, reattached his leg, and then put his pants back on. By the time he was finished, a sizable crowd had gathered in the City Hall foyer.

A valuable lesson can be gleaned from my father's experience – the easiest way to draw a crowd is to drop your pants in public.

We have seen this truth demonstrated time and again, from Lady Godiva, to Madonna, to Kim Kardashian. I don't mean to imply that seeing my father in his briefs is equivalent to seeing an attractive pop icon, but they both demonstrate how to gather a crowd. In my father's case it was in the foyer of city hall but for others it is on Internet websites and checkout line magazines.

All of this is based on a fundamental tenet of human nature. We are attracted to sensational, unusual, bizarre, and tragic events. Everyone likes a good show. Accidents always draw a crowd, not because everyone wants to help but because everyone wants to see. Do something out of this world and folks will come. Now days, it's even a little more effective if you sprinkle it with some sex.

It is the way some do church growth. It is no longer good enough to gather on Christmas Eve, light a few candles and worship the birth of our Savior. No, we need live camels and donkeys, laser light shows, extravagant gift giveaways, and Hollywood-type productions. Sure, you can congregate a handful of people to study the spiritual warfare passage in Ephesians, but what if you drive an army tank on stage for the Sunday morning show. Many in the church have figured out the best way to attract a crowd is to do something like dropping your pants.

There appears to be a great deal of "pants-dropping" happening at church today. Several churches are getting in the practice of sponsoring cage fights. The sometimes violent displays are very appealing to young men. I guess the rationale is to beat the hell out of people so they can find Jesus. After an hour or so of techno music and dancing, a Catholic church in Sweden hopes young people will be open to the Gospel. On Easter Sunday, a church in Corpus Christi gave away sixteen cars, fifteen flat screen televisions and other stuff totaling two million dollars worth. The intent was to attract people who would not normally attend.

It all pales in comparison to what happened just down the road from me recently. Normally I would not mention the name of the person involved in such an embarrassing event, but he went to great lengths to make sure folks know about it, so I will help him out. Ed Young of Fellowship Church and his wife climbed up to the roof of their church building and spent twenty-four hours together in bed. I don't know why there is a bed on the church roof but apparently it is there.

In a stunt reminiscent of flag pole sitting from early in the 20th century, Ed and his wife spent twenty-four hours in the bed. Alvin "Shipwreck" Kelly originated flag pole sitting and his initial foray lasted thirteen hours and thirteen minutes, far short of the twenty-four hours of non-stop sex by the Youngs. Unlike Kelly in 1924, the Youngs broadcast their adventure live on the Internet.

All of this is carefully orchestrated to coincide with the release of Ed Young's latest book, "Sexperiment." It seems this is nothing more than a marketing stunt to drive customers to Amazon where they can purchase the book for $21.95. As usual, it's all about the money. Don't we have a term for those who use sex for money?

Young is more than fifty years old so hopefully he got a prescription for Viagra before making that climb to the church roof. Hey, next time we might get the pharmaceutical company to sponsor the event and generate an even bigger payday. After all, God wants us to have good sex. In Young's own words, sex is about "recreation and enjoyment." It seems only natural that God would approve of popping a couple of little blue pills to heighten the enjoyment. I hope they had a doctor on call in case he had one of those four hour problems.

I've heard more than one Youth Minister tell me that their greatest fear was finding a couple of high school kids in their youth group having sex in the church basement. Now it seems they should be even more concerned about the kids finding the pastor and his wife having sex on the church roof. It's not all bad news though; at least the pastor is not gay.

Call me old fashioned, but I have a difficult time understanding why we need to have a bed at church. I've seen pictures of Young's house and it appears there are plenty of bedrooms to be had. What's he going to tell his kids when he and his wife walk out the front door on Friday night, "We'll see you in twenty-four hours, your Mom and I are going up to the church for some fun" as he gives a subtle wink. Talk about being scarred for life - I hope they have a counselor standing by.

Church members will probably need to turn off the parental controls on their Internet browser before they visit the church website. I wonder if you will need to verify that you are twenty-one years old before viewing the pastor's sermons?

Another thing – how does he get his wife to go along with this stuff? It's quite common for guys to brag about their sexual exploits but usually women are a little more discreet, especially a pastor's wife. To listen to your pastor's wife talk about her bedroom exploits is only slightly more comfortable than listening to your mother have the same conversation.

I guess the biggest question I have is what does this have to do with lifting up Jesus? Unless there are some huge gaps in the New Testament record, Jesus never had sex. The Apostle Paul suggested that if you are not currently married you should stay single to avoid the complications of marital life. I am not suggesting that sex is a bad thing nor do I mean to imply the Bible has nothing to offer on the subject. But please, can we be a little more discreet?

The reason the church is spouting out so much garbage is because we are searching for the right magnet, one that is big enough to fill up our sanctuaries with people who need Jesus. However, the whole point of this book is that we do not need a better magnet to attract people – we already have Jesus. Listen to what He said about Himself: "*And I, if I am lifted up from the earth, will draw all men to Myself.*" (John 12:32)

We don't need professional entertainers, men in cages punching each other, a pastor and his wife in bed on the church roof, or giant giveaways. We already have Jesus and He is enough. Folks, by their lack of participation, keep telling us they are unhappy with the church and we respond by trying to do it better or be more bizarre. These same folks who are no longer interested in our churches also tell us they still have respect for Jesus.

The answer seems simple enough. Quit doing the things that turn people away and start lifting up Jesus. When Jesus instructed us to lift Him up there seems to be two ways to understand how this is done. Obviously it is a reference to being lifted up on the cross. In fact, in a previous conversation with Nicodeumus (John 3), Jesus likened it to the experience of Moses lifting the serpent in the wilderness. All those who looked to the raised serpent were saved. Thus, when Jesus was hoisted on the cross He was lifted up and all who turn to Him will be saved.

Yet there is another sense in which Jesus can be lifted up and that is to give Him prominence, to hold Him up before others to see. It is the idea of drawing attention to Him and pointing people to who He is and what He does. It is like introducing someone to a friend and then getting out of the way and let them become friends with each other. I have a friend, Scott, who is very qualified in a specific field of study. I have another friend who recently funded a Teaching Chair in that same area of study at a local seminary. It seemed obvious that they needed to meet one another. I got them together, made the introduction and got out of way. I knew if they talked they would figure things out.

Sure enough, after their conversation, my friend who had funded the position came and asked if I thought Scott would be a good candidate. There was no need for me to try to convince or persuade, all I needed to do was bring them together, to introduce them and let them figure it out. Within a few months, Scott was a full professor at the seminary.

I think it was important that I didn't try to maneuver a relationship, pass around a resume, or put together a PowerPoint presentation. All I needed to do was introduce a friend to someone who could meet his need.

This helps me understand the task of the church and the attractive power of Jesus. We don't need to produce large crowds. All we need to do is tell our friends about a Friend. In my sixty years of life, I can count on one hand the number of people who have attempted to introduce me to Jesus. I am frequently invited to attend the show down at the church but I hear very little about Jesus.

It might be an amazing thing if we stopped producing extravaganzas and started lifting up Jesus. He claims to have the power to draw all to Him. Either He was mistaken or else we are not lifting Him up.

THE SHAPING POWER OF CHRIST

"It is better to live in a corner of a roof than in a house shared with a contentious woman" (Proverbs 21:9). This proverb is actually included two times in the Book of Proverbs so there must be some significance in the words.

In ancient Israel, the corner of a roof referred to a spot on top of the house where people would sit to enjoy the sun on a cool day or perhaps even find a place to sleep on an exceptionally warm evening. It was not a Master Suite on the upper floor of a house, but literally a corner in the open air. It might be a pleasant location occasionally but certainly not a place you would want to live day in and day out.

But we are told, it is better to live in that rooftop corner than inside the house with a "contentious" woman. Other translations use the terms "nagging" or "quarreling." I certainly don't mean to imply that only women can be nagging or quarrelsome. In fact, some of the most nagging people I have known have been men. A nag is someone who continually finds faults with others. If you have lived with a nagging person you know that it is virtually impossible to please them. Regardless of what you do they are quick to remind you that it could have been done better or differently. They make life very unpleasant.

Before I get on my high horse and gripe about nagging people, I must confess that I have been guilty myself.

All of us have at times. The reason we tend to nag others is because we get to thinking that we know what is best and we really want to help others. If they would just do it this way or live their life this way everything would be better. It is one of the consequences of fallen human nature to believe that we know best and that our way of doing things is the right way. When we couple that with our concern for helping others, it turns into nagging.

It is hard to get it through our heads that nagging does not change people. The reality is that it is impossible to change another person. We can encourage them, help them, pray for them, scold them, nag them, and do numerous other things to them, but we cannot change them. The ability to change another person belongs only to God.

If that is true, why do we try so hard to change one another at church? When someone comes to our church and they have a sin, our first reaction is to feel like we need to help them change. For example, a young woman comes to church, even attends for several weeks, and we discover that she is living a lifestyle we know is displeasing to God. (How we think we know the mind of God is another matter.) Often, someone in the church will take it upon themselves (or perhaps even the church leadership) and confront her with her need to change. We might even offer to tell her how it should be done.

Her problem is that she is living on the wrong side of our fence (see earlier chapter on fences) and we simply want to help her get on the right side. After all, isn't that what God wants?

Likely what will happen with this young woman is that she will feel angry and judged and walk away from the church, armed with another bad experience. Or, she might feel guilty and hopeless because she is not capable of living up to our standards and she will also walk away. If you don't think this is the case then you don't know enough people who live different lifestyles. If you find someone who is struggling with life, it is likely they will tell you that at some point they turned to the church for help but what they got was "nagging."

We all need to step out of our comfort zones frequently and discover how the rest of the world lives and thinks. We need to put ourselves in experiences and in relationship with people who will challenge our thinking and stretch our faith. We need to allow other people to find God in their own way and then allow Him to do the changing.

Personally, I'm thinking about changing generations. I was born a baby-boomer; on the older end of the scale, in fact. In case you are wondering, I was born in the last quarter of 1950. I have always been proud of being a baby-boomer. We had the potential of being a great generation, and we started well.

We were curious and questioning. We didn't trust anything blindly. We produced some great innovations. We brought personal computers into everyone's home. We invented the Internet (probably not Al Gore), and we laid the foundation for those after us to take technology to unimagined places. We drove the economy to record levels, providing more people with more stuff than anyone would have ever dreamed.

But, I'm not thinking about abandoning my generation because of our lack of successes. I am more concerned about our failures. Take politics for example. We lived through the megalomania of Nixon and the double-digit inflation of Carter. All the time, we were just waiting until one of our own became leader of the world. How disappointing has that been? Since we have been in charge, the White House has become a "red-light district," we have sent our young men and women to fight several wars, and America is hated by everyone in the world.

Things are no better when it comes to our religion. We have turned evangelism into marketing, worship into entertainment, and giving into fund-raising. We have turned God into Santa Claus, Jesus into a Republican, and the Holy Spirit into Dr. Phil. In our families, we have spoiled our children and abandoned our commitments to one another.

You might say that I am just being cynical, and perhaps you are right. However, how can you disagree with my assessment that we have not done well in some very important areas. I really think there must be a better way. I am ready to try something different.

It is time that we try something different with the church. We need to strive for things like authenticity, acceptance, honesty, sincerity, relationships, caring, openness and love. Things that should be frequent experiences in the church, but they are often lacking.

I am not saying that we baby-boomers have made a mess of things and the younger adults have gotten everything right. We have done, and continue to do, some very good things; and they have much to learn.

What I am admitting is that I am ready to try something different.

As a generation, baby-boomers turned our backs on our parent's view of the world. They made strong commitments; we chase every new fantasy. They were gatherers; we have become consumers. I am tired of being a good consumer and teaching others how to be good consumers.

We have even become known as Christian consumers. If you don't think that is the case, go to your neighborhood Christian bookstore and you will learn how to market to Christian consumers. Politicians see us as a group of potential voters if they will just say the right things and take certain positions. We even market our churches – "If you want exciting worship, caring fellowship, and a sermon to make you feel good, come to our church!"

One of my favorite contemporary theologians is Marva Dawn. She wrote these words about the modern church:

> . . . some pastors and musicians dispensed less truth instead of more, becoming therapeutic instead of theological; with the proliferation of entertainments, some worship leaders sacrificed content for form and confused worship with evangelism and evangelism with marketing.

The result is that everyone is marketing to me in the name of Christ – my politicians, my bookstore, and even my church. But, I can't be too critical, because it seems to work with us baby-boomers. We pick our churches like we pick our cell phone service – sign up with the one that best meets our needs.

I have concluded that I don't want a church that meets my needs. I don't need music that makes me clap my hands, a sermon that makes me feel good, or a small group that pats me on the back. I want a place where I can worship God and love the unlovable.

Let me tell you about an amazing experience I had at church a few years ago that captures what I am talking about. I realize it is a risk to do so, because some of you will think it is wrong or that I am crazy. I will not tell you the name of the church because some of you will insist that they be disciplined (shame on you).

During a time they refer to as "open mike," a young man stood up and read a poem. It was a poem filled with hurt and rejection. When he finished, he announced to the church that he was "bi-sexual." It was obviously difficult for him to say, and he was not offering to repent. He took his seat and there was silence.

Two of the pastors (leaders, elders, whatever) of the church went to the microphone and assured the young man that he was loved and welcome. They also challenged the rest of us not to criticize or tease him. As they spoke, a young woman in the church went and whispered in the young man's ear and kissed him on the cheek.

My faith was certainly stretched by the experience. It was obviously the topic of conversation on the way home. Late that night I sent an email to the pastor and here is part of his response:

It seems to me that most often Christendom has gone to one extreme or the other. It's either like the Corinthian church where we say that we love you no matter what and you can do whatever you want or we take the position of the Pharisees and the only way "IN" is to be perfect and we'll be quick to judge anyone who is not.

Our goal is to somehow pull off what Jesus did with the woman caught in adultery. All of our offenses are primarily against God and so her's was a slap in the face to Jesus. In the context of that he looked on her with love and compassion and said, "I (who by the way, have every right) choose not to condemn you but to love and accept you." However, he didn't leave it at that. He also added the, "Now, go and sin no more." That's the tricky part ... how do you pull off both of those?

I don't know how well we did that last night ... but fortunately, we're on a long-term relationship with (the young man). We are very blessed and humbled in that we have earned his trust for him to be willing to take such a huge risk with us.

Part of me would love to live in denial and just put on the pretty "church mask" and show up and pretend that everything is ok. Oh, the bliss of ignorance! The other part, the bigger part, is so grateful to be part of people's lives in the real issues they face day to day.

I wish I had that much wisdom when I was his age. There is something about that church that allowed the young man to share himself. Sure, it is ugly. But, now they can love him honestly. It is up to God to change his heart, not the church.

I have been in a lot of churches in my lifetime. I don't know if I have ever been in one that could have done what this church accomplished – right in front of everyone, during a worship service.

Early church father, Tertullian, in a celebrated passage written in his "Apologeticus" said these words about the pagan's view of the church:

'Behold,' they say, 'how they love one another!' Yea, verily this must strike them; for they hate each other. 'And how ready they are to die for one another!' Yea, truly; for they are rather ready to kill one another. And even that we call each other 'brethren,' seems to them suspicious for no other reason, than that, among them, all expressions of kindred are only feigned.

The reputation of the church is no longer, "how they love one another!" Today, it is more likely to be, "how they despise everyone who is different!"

I think the reason we have become the way we are is that we believe it is our responsibility to change others. We have forgotten that only Jesus can change another person. Once we arrange our approach to that truth, we will then be set free to love people for who they are.

I attended college and seminary with a friend named Charlie. He was a rather unusual guy, but once you got to know him it was obvious he had great potential. However, he was very rough around the edges. His wife claimed that she married Charlie, not for who he was but for who he could become. They had some serious early struggles because she was waiting for him to change and he wasn't real interested in doing so.

Our love for others who come to our churches is often that same kind of love – we love them for who they can become, not for who they are. The problem is that most of them are not interested in becoming what we want them to be so they are very difficult to love. They soon leave feeling judged, criticized, and condemned because that is exactly what we have done.

It is not easy to leave the change up to Jesus. He might not do it like we want and he will probably not do it as soon as we want. That means we must go to church with folks who are way different from us, perhaps some of them even make us uncomfortable. In my experience, Christians dealing with people living in "obvious sin" most often refer to the story of Jesus and the woman caught in adultery. Let's look at that passage for a moment.

> *But Jesus went to the Mount of Olives. Early in the morning He came again into the temple, and all the people were coming to Him; and He sat down and began to teach them. The scribes and the Pharisees brought a woman caught in adultery, and having set her in the center of the court, they said to Him, "Teacher, this woman has been caught in adultery, in the very act. Now in the Law Moses commanded us to stone such women; what then do You say?" They were saying this, testing Him, so that they might have grounds for accusing Him. But Jesus stooped down and with His finger wrote on the ground. But when they persisted in asking Him, He straightened up, and said to them, "He who is without sin among you, let him be the first to throw a stone at her." Again He stooped down and wrote on the ground. When they heard it, they began to go out one by one, beginning with the older ones, and He was left alone, and the woman, where she was, in the center of the court. Straightening up, Jesus said to her, "Woman, where are they? Did no one condemn you?" She said, "No*

one, Lord." And Jesus said, "I do not condemn you, either. Go. From now on sin no more." John 8:1-11)[1]

Most of us do not like to have our sins exposed in public. We go to great lengths to keep others from learning about our faults and misbehaviors. After committing a crime, many criminals create worse problems for themselves by trying to hide their crimes. Although we know we are sinners, and we are aware that everyone else knows that we sin, it is still a very private matter.

The woman described in John's Gospel suffered the embarrassment of having her sin made very public. Although her sin, adultery, may not be our sin, her embarrassment over being made a public spectacle is certainly one that we all fear. Ultimately, there are no secret sins.

We know nothing of the background of this woman before she was thrust onto the ground in front of Jesus. Since she was accused of adultery, she was obviously married, or at the least, betrothed to be married. Her body already belonged to someone else. In the act of adultery, she gave her body to the wrong person.

It might have been a one-time act of passion, a spur of the moment fall into the arms of the wrong lover. She might have been a young woman, unfulfilled by an

---

[1] It is possible that your Bible has a footnote or some indication that this passage (John 7:53-8:11) is not contained in the original version of John's Gospel. In fact, some ancient manuscripts include it in the Gospel of Luke. Most scholars conclude that the story was not originally written by John in the place where we have it today. However, no one questions the authenticity. Perhaps more than any other encounter with Jesus, we find in this story, a great expression of the mercy of our Lord.

uncaring husband who spent his nights with friends and family rather than at home with his wife. We can understand how she might have been tempted into the arms of a long-time friend, or perhaps swept off her feet by a handsome stranger.

It is possible that she and her lover maintained a long-term relationship, hidden for months, or years, from her husband's knowledge. Maybe she was simply a prostitute, abandoned by a slacker husband, or widowed by a man cut down in the prime of life. We really know nothing about her background. What we do know, from the testimony of witnesses, is that she was guilty of adultery.

The telling of the story by John gives the impression that the woman was snatched from her bed, drug through the dusty city streets, and thrown to the ground at Jesus' feet. As she slouched in the dirt, her flesh was barely covered by the blanket she clutched as her accusers hustled her out of the bedroom. They were obviously not concerned with the woman's modesty. The clear implication is that she was simply a pawn, being used to put Jesus in a conundrum.

The reason we expose the sins of others is because it allows us to feel good about ourselves. Make no mistake, publicly embarrassing someone else is always a selfish act. Some people will claim that they are really seeking the truth, or that they are doing it for the good of the sinner, but the truth is that such exposure is very unloving. When we really love someone, we do not expose their sins. Love motivates us to do the exact opposite – to keep their sins from view.

This was the chief difference between the scribes and Pharisees, and Jesus. They were simply using the woman; Jesus actually loved the woman. To the accusers, the woman was like a Styrofoam cup, to be disposed after use. If they had been serious about the sin of adultery they would have behaved much differently. Adultery is one of those unique sins that requires the cooperation of a partner. If their concern was stamping out the sin, they would have also brought the partner.

Their failure to bring the man has left this story open to speculation about his identity. Some have suggested that he was a participant in the plan to trap Jesus. His assignment was to lure the woman into a compromising position, alert the others, and disappear. Our opinion of the scribes and Pharisees allows us to accept the plausibility of this theory. They were not above manipulating a situation for their own purposes.

If the adultery participating man was not a part of the plot, he must have considered himself very fortunate. At the very least, he should have his sin publicly exposed alongside his female partner. It would have been just as appropriate for the eyes of the crowd to view his shame. However, since he did not serve their purpose, the scribes and Pharisees paid no attention as he slithered away from the scene of the crime. In the end, he might have been the biggest loser in this entire episode. Because he escaped the accusations, he missed the opportunity to encounter the Savior.

The adulterous woman met the Savior. It was not a meeting that she expected, nor was it planned. No one would purposely come to the feet of the Son of God, barely wrapped in a blanket, with hair disheveled from a night of sex and sleep. A thin layer of sand, from the city streets, covered more of her body than did the coveted blanket. She was afraid, confused, and crying, as she felt the penetrating stares from the curious crowd that gathered around Jesus. From her perspective there was nothing but chaos. Screaming and hollering drowned out the gasps of disbelief.

"Bring her over here, quickly, over here!" is what one man kept ordering.

She didn't know what they were doing, but it was apparent that they were fulfilling a plan. She did know that her sin was being exposed, right on the city streets, where everyone could see and hear.

The dragging stopped, the dust began to settle, and the sound of screaming was slowly replaced by incoherent whispers. After a few minutes, when the commotion was calmed, the dominating voice of one of her accusers penetrated into everyone's ears.

"Teacher, this woman has been caught in adultery, in the very act," he said with planned precision. "Now in the law, Moses commanded us to stone such women; what then do you say?"

As he spoke, the crowd hushed. When he finished they began to murmur to one another. They had been frequently amazed at Jesus' teaching. He was becoming well-known as a rabbi with a unique perspective on the law of God. But, there was no way to solve this problem. In this theological chess match, it seemed like the scribes and Pharisees had him checkmated.

The obvious answer, at least to a casual reader of the law, was that Jesus would have to agree that the woman should be stoned. Yet, if Jesus took this position, then He would face two problems. First, He would lose his popularity among the common people. The majority of folks attracted to Jesus were classified as sinners, just like this adulterous woman (and you and me as well). These non-religious people would have walked away from Jesus, disillusioned by His strict adherence to burdensome legalism.

Second, to side with the scribes and Pharisees would create problems with the Roman authorities. If Jesus participated in a public stoning then He could expect wrath from these occupying pagans. They did not permit the Jews to administer the death penalty without official permission.

The other possibility posed by the scribes and Pharisees was for Jesus to absolve the woman of any guilt. The Pharisees had listened to Jesus' teaching and this is probably the direction they anticipated. Once Jesus chose this course of action, they stood ready to accuse Him of breaking the Law of Moses. Leviticus was very clear when it said, "the adulterer and the adulteress shall surely be put to death" (Leviticus 20:10).

These Pharisees exposed a very dangerous perspective. They were willing to sacrifice this woman's life for their own purposes. They were not concerned about her welfare; they were only interested in finding support for their own position. When our beliefs take precedence over people, the result will be rock throwing. These religious rulers abused this woman, misused the Law of Moses, and criticized Jesus for their own gain.

I have a friend who was married for about a month and then divorced. The marriage was never consummated sexually, and they never even lived together. All of this happened before he became a Christian. Today this man is a pastor. It is amazing how many rocks are thrown at him by Christians as a result of this blundered marriage. These religious zealots will even ignore the fact that he is now a devoted husband and father, a model to be respected.

Anytime we give priority to our opinion over people the result will be rock throwing. God did not give the law as a religious tool to judge and criticize others. He gave it to point us to our need for forgiveness and salvation. We must also be careful not to use God's law as an instrument for justifying our own lifestyle. Rock throwers are notorious for ignoring their own sins, and highlighting the sins of others. This woman was about to be the recipient of a stoning, as it appeared Jesus would be helpless to change the course of events.

It is likely that neither this woman, nor anyone else in the crowd, had ever actually witnessed a stoning. Not only was the authority for administering the death penalty withheld from the Jews by the Romans, the religious leaders were not anxious to kill sinners. Their purpose was to discredit Jesus in the minds of the mindless masses. Even though she did not know the particulars of a stoning, she was certain it was something to be avoided.

To most of us, the idea of stoning conjures up the image of a victim being lined up against a wall, as a large crowd pelts them with chunks of granite. As painful as that seems, that is not an accurate reflection of the ancient practice of stoning. In Jewish procedure, the culprit was stripped, with hands tied behind the back. They were placed on a scaffold nearly a dozen feet in the air. The first witness, and testifier against the accused, pushed the sinner over the ledge. If the fall produced death, the punishment was ended. However, if death did not occur, the next witness dropped a very large stone on the breast of the convicted. This "first stone" usually produced the sought for consequence of death.

From her slouched position at the feet of Jesus, this woman sat motionless, dazed. So much out of the ordinary had happened to her in the past few moments that she was in shock. Even if she were not afraid to open her mouth, she had no idea what to say. How could she possibly defend herself against so many witnesses, and the physical evidence of her appearance?

Although she might not have recognized Jesus as the new celebrity in town, it was quickly apparent that He was the center of everyone's focus. She had been cast down at His feet. The question of punishment had been directed to His attention. The anticipation of the crowd was tuned in to His response. She was smart enough to realize that life or death for her depended on His determination.

Even though I am confident that this adulterous woman feared for her life, I am unconvinced that she would have ever been executed. The intent of the scribes and Pharisees was to disgrace Jesus. They only wanted to trap him, and once His answer was uttered, they would have walked away from the woman – mission accomplished. The greatest danger she faced – of having her sin publicly exposed – was behind her. However, the fear of death can be just as disconcerting as the possibility of death.

The woman cowered in fear at Jesus' feet. The crowd clamored in anticipation of Jesus' answer. The scribes and Pharisees relished the sweet smell of victory. Jesus did very little.

He stooped down and began to scribble in the dirt with his index finger. I would like to join the many commentators and speculators at this point and offer my opinion about Jesus' writing, but I have no opinion. I have studied a myriad of suggestions on the subject – from those who use this to teach the importance of writing down our thoughts before we speak, to others who use it to teach that we should follow Jesus' example and never write down anything that can be preserved longer than scribbles in the sand. Obviously, we do not know what Jesus wrote. If those standing at His side read the writing, they remained silent.

Jesus wrote in the dirt and the anticipation must have been paralyzing. Was this the time when Jesus was finally baffled? How would He respond to such a precarious predicament?

He said nothing, so they kept asking.

"What do you say, Jesus! Should we stone her like Moses said?"

Still no response.

"Some teacher you are! You can't even answer the simplest question," taunted the accusers.

Finally, after what seemed like eternity for the woman at his feet, Jesus stood erect and turned to face His questioners.

"He who is without sin among you," He uttered in a clear, firm voice, "let him be the first to throw a stone at her."

The entire crowd remained silent, as Jesus stooped down and resumed His writing in the ground. Perhaps some of the younger, more impertinent participants let out a half-hearted snicker at Jesus' words, but no one had anything to say. They were all stunned – as silent as the stones they were anxious to hurl.

Jesus essentially offered an invitation to those who had witnessed the adultery. Remember the Jewish practice of stoning meant that the one who cast the first stone is the one who does the killing.

"If you have no sin in your life, then go ahead, you be the one to kill this woman!" It is fascinating, that the only one present in that dusty city courtyard who met the qualifications that Jesus established, was Jesus Himself. He was the only one without sin.

As is always the case, after Jesus speaks there is nothing more that needs to be said. It was only a few minutes before the older, wiser accusers slowly turned and walked away from the impromptu trial. They were soon followed by the others. Even the spectators realized that the show was over and it was time to go home.

In a master stroke, Jesus had turned the table on his opponents. It was a move that would have left any chess master in awe. As they sometimes say in athletics, He snatched victory from the jaws of defeat.

It did not take long for everyone to depart, and Jesus was left alone with the adulterous woman. We don't know where the disciples were, the storyteller does not give us this detail. All we have is a very personal, face-to-face encounter between Jesus and a sinner. That should not surprise us because that is why Jesus came. He wants to meet sinners face-to-face.

Throughout the entire story, the woman has been talked about, but no one talked to her. When the accusers left, Jesus changed that as He spoke to her, "Woman, where are they? Did no one condemn you?"

How foolish it is to stand before Jesus with words of condemnation of others on our lips. How can anyone be an accuser when speaking to the all-knowing Messiah? When we stand in Jesus' presence, we are confronted with our own sinfulness, not the faults of others. That is exactly what happened. Everyone left that day with full awareness of their own sin.

The adulterous woman replied with a very short phrase, "No one, Lord." This woman, still wrapped in the blanket of immorality, saw all of her accusers vanish. Even the One qualified to make accusations, chose to say, "I do not condemn you, either. . ."

Once he had dispatched her accusers and delivered her from danger, Jesus then acknowledged her existence. This is the beginning of grace, to be acknowledged by the Son of God. This is the Good News of the Gospel; God knows us and our problems.

After recognizing the woman, Jesus said, "Neither do I condemn you..." These are the most precious words any person can hear. There is no better news than the report that God does not condemn us. The sinful ones were prepared and anxious to throw stones, but the sinless One refused to offer condemnation.

This is what set Jesus apart from the scribes and Pharisees. He is not out to condemn, but to redeem. As we strive to relate to others this is an important model to follow. Condemnation is easy, redemption takes effort. Instead of throwing stones we should be reaching out in forgiveness.

Yet, we must also realize that grace is not easy on sin. Jesus said, "Go. From now on sin no more."

This is what it means to love the sinner and hate the sin. Jesus is teaching us how to relate to sinners. It means to take a person who is judged and abused by others, love them, and set them on a redemptive course.

God does not forgive us and then set us free to continue in our sin. That would be grace which is powerless. When He forgives, God sets us free to amend our ways. When we throw rocks at those caught in sin, we destroy this whole process of grace.

In my office I have a softball-sized rock which has the Scripture reference "John 8:7" printed on the side. It is a reminder to me of this verse. God often directs my attention to this stone before I speak. Sometimes I have even directed another person's attention to it when they get carried away with criticism about others.

A stone is not symbolic of grace. The symbol of grace is the open arms of Jesus as he lifted this woman to her feet and set her free from condemnation. In every relationship we have the opportunity of administering judgment or grace. If we stand before another person as judge, then we deny them the opportunity of grace.

There was a sizable number of people watching, waiting to see Jesus' response. They were also closely watching the religious leadership. People are watching closely today to see how Christians respond to sinners and their sin. When they observe us throwing stones at one another, and at others, they expect to receive the same treatment. Consequently, they have no desire to be a part of that kind of fellowship.

The crowds who stood behind Jesus and watched His response to the adulterous woman saw something very appealing. They observed One who would love them and be able to help them. This is why the people came to Jesus. It is why people are still attracted to Jesus. Tragically, that is not the way we are doing church nowdays.

It is usually an overstatement to say that everyone is doing something but it does seem like everyone on the Internet recently has been talking about gays and gay marriage. It seems about half the posts I notice on Facebook and Twitter deal with the subject and most of the blogs I frequently read have all taken a stance on the issue. Of course, all the politicians have stated their position since it is an election year. Even people who typically say nothing about political or moral concepts are diving into the fray.

I don't mind a good debate, even if it concerns a hot potato (do I use "o" or "oe," I can't remember?). Of course, religion and politics can always be counted on to lead to such a discussion. In this case, it seems like we have both of them wrapped up together and that is probably why everyone has an opinion.

But here's the problem. Christians have become so involved in the debate and so vocal and strident in our position it is possible that it has become a stumbling block. George Barna, the guy Christians look to for help in understanding the world, reports that ninety-one percent of non-Christians pick the term anti-homosexual to describe Christianity. In other words, this is the first thing they think of when we use the word "Christian." By the way, not far behind were the terms "judgmental" (eighty-seven percent) and "hypocritical" (eighty-five percent).

That means when non-believers notice the fish symbol on the back of your SUV they immediately think you are an anti-homosexual, judgmental, hypocrite. That's a lot to overcome if you plan to stop and tell them about Jesus.

Some of you are proud to be known as anti-homosexual, but is that really the first thing you want people to think about you? When they pronounce the final words over your grave, do you really want the preacher to say, "Here lies Bob. He was a fine Christian man, the best anti-homosexual in the county!"

It is easy to quickly dismiss me as being flippant and extreme, but these survey numbers expose a serious problem we have created for ourselves. They are simply describing the picture of Christianity that we have painted. I realize some of the blame goes to extremists like the fruitcakes at Westboro Church in Kansas who are sandpaper harsh. Their clamoring means that the rest of us must make up the difference in presenting a different version of the Christian faith.

The issue is not really homosexuality but about how we represent ourselves to those who need to meet Jesus. As the church, we are the body of Christ. We are His hands and His feet. We are the tangible expression of Jesus in the world. What they know about Him is what they see in us.

When they hear us constantly arguing about issues, condemning gay people, spewing hatred toward politicians in the wrong party, and accusing everyone who does not believe like we do of being evil then what else are they to think. They are drawing the obvious conclusion that we are anti-something, judgmental, and hypocritical.

The accusation that Christians are hypocritical is very interesting to me. Most people who have any knowledge at all about the Christian faith know that it is about grace and forgiveness. The very center of the faith is that Christ died to pay the price for our sin so we could be forgiven. So here we are, forgiven sinners, yet we often go around criticizing and condemning other sinners. That sounds hypocritical to me.

Hurling stones of judgment toward others is not a new problem. The story of Jesus and the woman caught in adultery is really a story about judging other people. The climax of the event is when Jesus says, "Let him who is without sin cast the first stone." Yet, the way people read that story today is to make what happens later the main point of the story. They like to focus on Jesus' words to the sinful woman, "Go and sin no more."

If we are honest, we must admit we are more like the Pharisees who want to condemn sinners than Jesus who wants to forgive sinners. We want to skip the forgiving part and get right to the stop doing it part. The problem is that people who have not experienced grace are not able to stop sinning. Consequently, all they hear from us is condemnation and straighten out your life – not very appealing words.

We have gotten ourselves in trouble because we have taken on a task that does not belong to us. For some reason we have the opinion that our duty is to straighten people out, to let them know when they are wrong and get them moving in the right direction. That is not the work of the church. We have been sent out to proclaim the Good News, which is not a message of condemnation and judgment. It is a message of forgiveness and hope.

I am not suggesting that we cannot take a stance against things we consider sinful, but that must not be our primary calling card. When ninety-one percent of non-believers identify us anti-anything, it is a problem.

The task before us is enormous. We must make a one hundred and eighty degree change of direction in the way we communicate our faith. We don't want folks to think we are negative, always against something. Instead, we want them to see the Christian faith as hope, forgiveness, and relationship with God. When they see the fish symbol on the back of your SUV their first reaction should be, "There is a person who cares about me!"

What About Heresy?

When you take down a fence, you run the risk of your dog getting out of the yard or the neighbor's dog getting into your yard. Frequently, the initial reaction when you speak of removing the circumference of the church is concern over allowing heresy in the church. It is good to let everyone in, but when you do, how do you keep false belief out? I don't know the answer but let me share an experience we had with our small congregation.

We had a young lady who had been a part of our fellowship from the beginning. As a seminary student she was studying to be a chaplain. Apparently one of the requirements for being hired as a chaplain is ordination by a church or religious group. We understood from the beginning that she was eager for our group to grow to the point where we felt comfortable ordaining a minister.

After a year or so, we felt like we were at that point and began looking into the process of making it happen. Since we were not a member of a traditional denomination we did not have a specified process to follow. We determined we would begin by asking her to share her faith and spiritual experience.

The young woman provided a couple of documents, one describing her faith and the other her call into ministry. As soon as I read them I knew we were in trouble. I forwarded them to Charlie and he had the same reaction. Upon reading her words, we were unsure about her faith. We hoped she was just a poor writer and unable to express her true thoughts. One of the things you learn in seminary is how to write page after page without really saying what you mean.

We arranged a meeting to discuss her beliefs and to share our concerns. It seemed the meeting went well and the young woman said she understood our concerns and agreed to do a rewrite, assuring us that we had just misunderstood her intention.

Throughout the process, we continually reminded her that our objective was to get to the point where we could ordain her. However, we also explained that we would not do so until everyone was comfortable with her expression of faith. We tried not to put words in her mouth and tell her what she needed to say or believe. We were also careful to assure her that the decision to pursue the process was entirely hers.

I was reminded of a seminary professor I had years ago. He said he never refused to officiate a wedding ceremony, although he did require every couple come to him for pre-marital counseling. The point was he would not marry them until he felt they were ready. He did have a few couples who realized after some time in counseling that they should either stay single or find another minister. It was their decision, not his.

That is similar to what we did with the young woman seeking ordination. We tried to keep pointing her to our faith in Christ, but she could not make that same leap. It was her decision not to be ordained by our congregation. We were willing to keep the process open as long as she was interested but we were unwilling to put anything other than Christ in the center of the process.

Not creating a circumference by building fences does not mean that every belief and practice is acceptable. Eliminating a circumference can only be successful as long as Christ is the center. If you remove Christ from the equation it is no longer a Christian church but something more like a Unitarian congregation. Lifting up Jesus and loving people is not license to believe and do whatever you want.

The only Jesus we know is the one we discover when reading the scriptures. Consequently, everything we teach and preach must come from God's Word. Each of our worship services at Bread Fellowship are built around this belief. We normally follow the Christian calendar as a means of keeping us rooted in the historical faith. The Lectionary also guides our sermons and discussions. This is important because it keeps our attention spread throughout all of God's Word – Old Testament history, Psalms and Writings, Gospels, New Testament History, Epistles, etc.

The intent is not to water down the Gospel in order to please everyone. The goal is to preach the Gospel in such a way that our proclamation and practices don't exclude those who are looking for Jesus. The greatest religious fence destroyer was Jesus Himself (just ask the Pharisees). He was able to proclaim the truth and welcome everyone who came to Him. That is what the church is to be about.

One of our obstacles is the size of our churches. When our obsession is with "church growth" then we gather in such large groups that heresy becomes very likely. Loss of intimacy contributes to heresy. It allows people to come and go and infect the congregation without leadership being aware of their false teaching. I'm not talking about legitimate differences in biblical interpretation. In our small congregation we have folks with a wide variety of theological presuppositions. We have some with a charismatic background, dispensationalists, mysticism, evangelical liberal, evangelical conservative, fundamentalist, and others. Yet, when we gather around the word of God we are able to discuss it with genuine care for one another, allow differing opinions without fighting, and we all typically walk away with a greater appreciation of Christ.

This would probably not be possible if our group were large. We are still able to know one another and allow time and provide opportunity for everyone to speak. It is possible to know what each believes and thinks about issues that come up. Consequently, it is much easier to recognize problems before they are allowed to infect the entire congregation.

In Matthew 13, Jesus told a parable that I think address this question of heresy among us.

> *"The kingdom of heaven may be compared to a man who sowed good seed in his field. But while his men were sleeping, his enemy came and sowed tares among the wheat, and went away. But when the wheat sprouted and bore grain, then the tares became evident also. The slaves of the landowner came and said to him, 'Sir, did you not sow good seed in your field? How then does it have tares?' And he said to them, 'An enemy has done this!' The slaves said to him, 'Do you want us, then, to go and gather them up?' But he said, 'No; for while you are gathering up the tares, you may uproot the wheat with them. Allow both to grow together until the harvest; and in the time of the harvest I will say to*

the reapers, "First gather up the tares and bind them
in bundles to burn them up; but gather the wheat into
my barn." (Matthew 13:24-30)

Later when they were alone, the disciples asked Jesus
to explain the meaning of this parable and He provided
this interpretation.

"The one who sows the good seed is the Son of Man,
and the field is the world; and as for the good seed,
these are the sons of the kingdom; and the tares are the
sons of the evil one; and the enemy who sowed them is
the devil, and the harvest is the end of the age; and the
reapers are angels. So just as the tares are gathered up
and burned with fire, so shall it be at the end of the age.
The Son of Man will send forth His angels, and they
will gather out of His kingdom all stumbling blocks,
and those who commit lawlessness, and will throw
them into the furnace of fire; in that place there will be
weeping and gnashing of teeth. Then the righteous will
shine forth as the sun in the kingdom of their Father.
He who has ears, let him hear." (Matthew 13:37-43)

Like the slaves in Jesus' story, we want to be weed
pullers. We tend to think it is our task to remove the
weeds so the church will be clean and pure. Jesus told
the parable to remind us the task of judging belongs
only to God.

False teaching will always be a problem for any church.
The best we can do is make sure that our own teaching
is the truth and do our best to encourage others to keep
Christ as the center of the message.

One Sunday evening as I was leading the service for
our small congregation. A young man and woman
came in just as we started so I had no opportunity to

visit with them before the service. They introduced themselves to the group and they participated in the activities for the evening. At the conclusion of the service, I immediately introduced myself and spoke with the young man named Todd.

He mentioned that he was a Baha'i and I had no idea what that meant so I asked for an explanation which he gladly provided. During the conversation I asked how he came to embrace this particular faith. He described how he was born and raised as a Jew. We talked about that for a few moments because it is rare to find a Jew in a Christian worship service. He described his family and spoke a little of his Jewish heritage.

Then he said something that really caught me off guard. He said when he got older he met Jesus. I must admit, my ears perked up. After he met Jesus he felt he needed to find a church. However, he had a difficult time deciding which church to attend. It seemed to him they all emphasized something different and none of them liked each other. They all seemed to be fighting one another. Consequently, he went looking for something else and that is how he found the Baha'i faith.

I was ashamed. It is the church that I have helped create that drove this young man away. It is the church that I have preached to for my entire adult life that made this new friend of Jesus go looking for something else. It is the church consisting of my friends and colleagues that felt it was more important to be "right" than to be loving.

We are doing something wrong. In our effort to look our best as we journey down the road of faith, we do not allow room for many who would like to take the trip with us. Sure, we tell them they can come along, but we are very clear on what they must do, how they must look, and what they must say. Imagine a young man who has just met Jesus but does not feel at home with Jesus' people.

I don't know much about Todd. Perhaps he is a difficult person (I have no reason to believe that), but I do know there is something wrong when he is driven away by our divisiveness. There has been much talk recently about young adults leaving the church. A young woman I enjoy reading, Rachel Held Evans, wrote these words about the church:

"Sometimes I need to be reminded that community is not about surrounding myself with people just like me; community is about loving my neighbor, whoever that neighbor may be. If the early church could hold together communities made up of Jews and Greeks, slaves and free, men and women, circumcised and uncircumcised, tax collectors and zealots, prostitutes and Pharisees, kosher believers and non-kosher believers, those who ate food sacrificed to idols and those who refused, I guess this evolution-accepting, hell-questioning, liberal-leaning feminist can worship Jesus alongside a Tea Party complementarian who thinks the earth is 6,000 years old and that Ghandi and Anne Frank are in hell. I'm not saying it will be easy, or even that it will work, but I think it's worth a try."

Shame on us because we have found a way to disagree on nearly everything – baptism (sprinkling or immersion), communion (open for all or closed to members only), scripture (inerrant or imperfect), women (be quiet and serve or fully equal), music (contemporary or traditional), buildings (functional or meaningful), worship (casual or liturgical), purpose (preach the gospel or feed the hungry), politics (Republican or Democrat), grace (faith alone or necessity of works), alcohol (abstinence or moderation), etc. etc. ad nauseam. It is not surprising that Todd could not decide on a church.

I hope we made Todd feel welcome. Hopefully we did and some day he will give Jesus another try. I don't want to pull out any more potential fruit because I thought it was a weed.

DISTRACTIONS TO AVOID

These twelve Jesus sent out after instructing them: "Do not go in the way of the Gentiles, and do not enter any city of the Samaritans; but rather go to the lost sheep of the house of Israel. And as you go, preach, saying, 'The kingdom of heaven is at hand.' Heal the sick, raise the dead, cleanse the lepers, cast out demons. Freely you received, freely give. Do not acquire gold, or silver, or copper for your money belts, or a bag for your journey, or even two coats, or sandals, or a staff; for the worker is worthy of his support." (Matthew 10:5-10)

At the age of 21, I sensed a call from God. A call from God is difficult to explain. I believe that every follower of Christ is called to evangelize, encourage, and explain the faith. But, some of us are the recipients of an assignment to give the majority of our lives to the work of the Gospel. In the thirty-nine years since that call, I have been a pastor for only about fourteen of those years. However, at any point of my life, if you ask me what I do, the answer has always been, "I'm a preacher!"

Preaching has not always paid the bills. I have made a living by being a salesman, consultant, denominational employee, writer, and book publisher. There have been times when I preached at three to five churches a week. There have been other times when I went three to five months between preaching opportunities. But it does not matter how often I preach, at any point of my life, if you ask me what I do, the answer has always been, "I'm a preacher!"

As I neared graduation from college, the head of the Religion department told me it would be very difficult for me to have an opportunity to pastor a church because of the wheelchair. At seminary, they excused me from preaching requirements and tried to steer me toward counseling, assuming that I was not physically able to preach. After thirteen successful years as a pastor, when it was time to move on, churches were not interested in even talking to me, in spite of glowing recommendations from Denominational leaders. However, it does not matter who thinks I can be a preacher, at any point of my life, if you ask me what I do, the answer has always been, "I'm a preacher!"

In spite of being frequently encouraged to pursue another career, it is the call of God that has shaped my life and determined my experiences. I have given my life to pursuing this call of God. I am enamored and overwhelmed with this call of God. I can honestly declare to you that I have exhausted my resources striving to be faithful to this call of God.

Because of that, not only am I deeply in love with following Jesus, but I am also deeply in love with the church – the Body of Christ – the physical presence of my Lord and Savior. Not only have I spent thirty-nine years studying Christ, I have also spent thirty-nine years studying the church. I have preached in nearly five hundred pulpits, provided extensive consultation with more than two hundred pastors, and read books and articles about the church vociferously. Needless to say, I have a lot of opinions about the church and church leaders.

To be honest, I am not very optimistic about the American church, which is exceptional for me since I tend to be the ultimate optimist. I not only see the glass as half full, I normally see it as flowing over the top. But, I am concerned about the church today and one of my primary concerns is that we have taken the call of God and turned it into a career. Perhaps this is the main reason the church has become what it is today.

The tenth chapter of Matthew is a record of Jesus' "call" to the Twelve. He called them and then sent them out with a task. Essentially, He gave them three tasks – to preach, heal, and trust. It is the work of the church and He has been calling men and women to the task ever since.

However, there is a prevalent trend in the church today to turn the call of God into a career. The dictionary definition of "career" is an occupation undertaken for a significant period of a person's life and with opportunities for progress. Basically, it is the answer to the question, "What do you want to be when you grow up?" The answer – I want to be a doctor, lawyer, baseball player, or preacher! It is a chosen profession for the purpose of providing an acceptable living. This is what happens when you turn a calling from God into a career.

When Jesus called the Twelve, He sent them out with a specific message – they were to preach "the kingdom of heaven is at hand." Theologians have written numerous volumes on the meaning of the kingdom of heaven and every seminary student will be asked to read some of them.

Since I must operate in the real world (not the world of academia) let me offer my real world understanding of this task. Obviously, "kingdom" speaks of the place where the King rules. Since it is the "kingdom of heaven" then it must be a reference to the place where God in heaven rules. The message that those who have been called are to proclaim is that the King of heaven is here.

Put yourself in first century Palestine, a land controlled by Caesar. Caesar is the king. If you are tending your field or shopping in the local market and you hear the announcement that "Caesar is here!" What would you do? It would make an immediate difference in your life. It would be a call to change what you are doing and possibly even change who you are. Something significant is about to happen!

The message of the church is that God, the creator and sustainer of the universe, has broken into history, sent His Son to open up a relationship with us, and is ready to radically alter our lives. It is a message of redemption and transformation. Like a first century Jew hearing that Caesar is coming down the road, it is a message that is shocking and will impact every area of our lives.

However, the announcement that the kingdom of heaven is here is no longer the primary message of the church. Instead it has been replaced with, "Let me tell you how to be successful." I did a Google search on the phrase, "How to be a successful Christian" and received nearly 41 million results. A search of the phrase "kingdom of heaven" did reveal 17 million results, but the first two pages concerned an R-rated movie about the 12th century Crusades.

The message has been changed for the purpose of making it less offensive and more acceptable to our 21st century world. The rationale is that in order to get large numbers of people into our church buildings, we must tell them what they want to hear. We call it "seeker-sensitive" but in reality it has become "seeker-driven."

- People want to know how to have a good family life so let's offer a series of sermons explaining what to do to make it happen.

- People are struggling with their finances so let's provide a workshop on managing your money.

- People are fighting depression so let's tell them how to overcome despair.

There is nothing wrong with any of these (and God knows I have done my share), but this is far less than the call we were given. We have been called to proclaim a much more important message than how to get along better in this world. Our message is an announcement to rearrange our lives according to a different world – there is a new king!

Jesus has asked us to invite folks to participate in a new world, but too often we try to help them be more comfortable in the existing world. The problem is that we have changed the message so that it sounds as if Christianity is nothing more than living the good life.

The method that Jesus gave to those He called is startling. They were to "heal the sick, raise the dead, cleanse the lepers, cast out demons," I'll be honest, this sounds more like a Benny Hinn crusade than anything I am comfortable with.

Apparently, the disciples were not as sophisticated as me. They went out preaching the kingdom and doing the works. Even before the Pentecostal gift of the Holy Spirit, the disciples proclaimed the message; using the methods they were given. Later we are told that they came back to report what they had seen.

I am going to say very bluntly that we do not see much sick-healing, dead-raising, unclean-cleansing, or demonic-outcasting today. What has happened? I think we have changed the method, primarily as a result of changing the message.

Once the message became more about being comfortable or successful rather than living in a different kingdom, it was easy to change the methods. If the message is nothing more than feel good and enjoy the best this world has to offer, we do not need to worry ourselves with healing, raising, and cleansing.

The method becomes more about comfort, entertainment, and education.

Since the message is to live the good life, it is necessary to provide comfort in a very uncomfortable world. We have turned our churches into sanctuaries where folks can go to have all their needs met without rubbing elbows with unpleasant people and challenging situations. The really "dynamic" churches provide all the sports leagues and entertainment venues for our children, relationship needs for the entire family, and all the God-stuff we need in our lives – all within the confines of a colorfully designed state of the art facility that makes us want to relax and stay a while.

While running the risk of being accused of taking the wrong side of the worship war, let me simply say that much of what happens when the church gathers today is more about entertainment than anything else. That is why we need monolithic congregations because providing the necessary entertainment is expensive.

A third aspect of our method is to educate. Listen to this quick list of real sermon topics:

- Living in the Sweet Spot of Success
- Taking Steps Toward Making Change
- Opening and Closing the Right Doors
- Avoiding Personal Burnout
- Twelve Keys to Abundant Living
- Save Me I'm Drowning in Debt

These sermons are typical of what happens in church today and it seems clear that our approach is to help people enjoy the here and now rather than arranging for life in a new kingdom.

The Hospice Movement began in this country in the 1960s. If you have ever had a loved one experience the process of dying under the watchful eye of a hospice professional, you know it is a valuable resource. Caring, well-trained people are there to help the entire family be comfortable and at ease with the entire process of dying and death. In my opinion, hospice care is a very good thing.

However, when it comes to the work of the church, providing hospice care is not a good thing. Yet, that is what I think we are doing. We are providing comfort for those who are dying in the wrong kingdom.

The final thing I want to mention about changing a call into a career is that it happens when we change our motive. This is really the heart of the message by Jesus in this passage.

Several years ago I was working with a young pastor and the subject of pastors from different generations came up. I was not quite old enough to be his father, but not far from it. He was curious about the approaches by pastors in different generations. I provided an example by asking a simple question – when you spoke to this church about being their pastor, did you ask about taking time off – vacation days, and days off, etc.?

Almost incredulously he said, "Of course, what's wrong with that!"

I quickly assured him there was probably nothing wrong with asking but it was a huge difference. I would have never asked. In fact, at his age, if a church was interested in me being their pastor, I would have never asked if they were even going to pay me.

There is nothing wrong with paying the preacher, in fact, Jesus makes it very clear in our text that the workman is worthy of payment. God provides, and for pastors He normally provides through a salary given by the church. But we have to be careful with motive.

When I was the pastor of a very small Texas Baptist church, every spring we would receive a survey from the state office. The survey sought for answers about pastor's salary and other benefits. The information was compiled by the Stewardship Department and then provided for help in putting together the church budget. I dutifully filed out my survey every year.

Later, when I went to work in the Stewardship Department, I learned that the survey was discontinued. I was told by the man in charge at the time that the survey created a problem. Pastors who were receiving a salary that was higher than the average were very upset. It seems that when their church leaders compared what they were paying their pastor compared to other churches, they wanted to make some changes.

When Jesus issued the call, He clearly said, "Do not acquire..." But, the evidence that we have turned this calling into a career is that it has been changed to, "What's in it for me?"

I'm going to be honest – choosing the ministry is not a bad career move. The pay is much better than it used to be, time off is good, most churches provide decent benefits, including insurance and retirement.

In times past, joining the army was seldom seen as a very good career choice for most people. However, times have changed. My youngest son, with a Master's Degree in Forensic Psychology, recently joined the army and quickly became a 2nd Lieutenant. He didn't make the decision because he wants to be Rambo, it is simply a good career move for what he wants to do.

The same is true for the modern church in America – it can be a good career move.

In Fort Worth where I live, there have been two very well known pastors caught up in scandals this past year over the ownership of a private jet. Some have turned the call of God into a very lucrative career. However, that is not my primary concern.

I am concerned about pastors of small and medium size churches who have locked themselves into a lifestyle that requires significant financial resources to maintain. They have put themselves in a position where they can no longer follow the call but must first seek a career. Their biggest concern has become doing whatever is necessary to insure that the offerings at church stay at a certain level. Decisions are made, not necessarily on what is best for the church but for what is most profitable.

I am also concerned about soon to be seminary graduates who will be tempted to allow the lure of "gold, or silver, or copper for your money belts, or a bag for your journey, or even two coats, or sandals, or a staff" distract them from the place where God has called them.

If you have been called, it is imperative that you keep yourself in a position that allows you to respond to that call. That means you must keep yourself free from relationships and obligations that will keep you from going and doing.

Recently, I read a very good book by Eugene Peterson, "The Pastor: A Memoir." He provides a valuable observation about what has taken place in the church.

...one of the most soul-damaging phrases that had crept into the Christian vocabulary is "full-time Christian work." Every time it is used, it drives a wedge of misunderstanding between the way we pray

and the way we work, between the way we worship and the way we make a living.

One of the achievements of the Protestant Reformation was a leveling of the ground between clergy and laity. Pastors and butchers had equal status before the cross. Homemakers were on a par with evangelists. But insidiously that level ground eroded as religious professionals claimed the high ground, asserted exclusive rights to "full-time Christian work," and relegated the laity to part-time work on weekends under pastoral or priestly direction. A huge irony— the pastors were hogging the show, and the laity were demeaned with the adjectives "mere," "only," or "just: ""He or she is just a layperson."

Most of what Jesus said and did took place in a secular workplace in a farmer's field, in a fishing boat, at a wedding feast, in a cemetery, at a public well asking a woman he didn't know for a drink of water, on a country hillside that he turned into a huge picnic, in a court room, having supper in homes with acquaintances or friends. In our Gospels, Jesus occasionally shows up in synagogue or temple, but for the most part he spends his time in the workplace. Twenty-seven times in John's Gospel Jesus is identified as a worker: "My Father is still working, and I also am working" (Jn. 5:17). Work doesn't take us away from God; it continues the work of God. God comes into view on the first page of our scriptures as a worker. Once we identify God in his workplace working, it isn't long before we find ourselves in our workplaces working in the name of God.[1]

[1] Peterson, Eugene H. (2011-02-22). The Pastor: A Memoir (pp. 280-281). Harper Collins, Inc. Kindle Edition.

If you have been by called, then you have been called to the work – the work of proclaiming the coming of God's kingdom by healing, raising, and cleansing. It is essentially the work of the church. However, if you put yourself in a position of needing the ministry to provide you with a certain lifestyle, it is likely that you will adapt the work of the church to serve your purpose. Here is the way that progression normally works:

- Need more money

- Attract larger crowds, they bring more money

- Provide services that draw larger crowds

- Need more money to pay for these services

One commitment that we have made at Bread Fellowship is not to allow this new fellowship to get in a position where we need large amounts of money. Neither Charlie nor I are dependent upon the church to put food on our table. There is no need, in a city like Fort Worth with hundreds of underused church buildings, for us to ever own property. Our hope is that Bread Fellowship will never be about the money. This does not mean we will not encourage folks to give and share (an important aspect of the Gospel message). It simply means we will try not to put ourselves in a position of needing something from the church that causes us to alter the task.

It has taken me until age 60 to arrive at this conclusion. I now understand that I am not dependent upon the church meeting my financial needs – that is God's work. Until you know this truth, you will not be free to follow the call that God has issued to you. "Do not acquire gold, or silver, or copper for your money belts, or a bag for your journey, or even two coats, or sandals, or a staff; for the worker is worthy of his support."

If we can avoid these kinds of distractions then we might be able to keep the fences down and welcome everyone who is attracted to Jesus. We will not be in a position where we need them and their money.

MAKING CHRIST MORE VISIBLE

A little more than a decade ago I came across a very memorable book. It was titled, "Out of the Saltshaker & into the World." It is one of those titles that actually captures the thesis of the book. The subject of the book is evangelism and the obvious point is that in order to be the salt of the world we must get out of our comfort zone and interact with the world.

Salt is a very powerful thing, packing a punch far beyond its size and appearance. If you are not convinced of the power of salt to make a difference, try adopting a "salt-free" diet. You will need to adjust to the taste of bland food. Salt has been used as a very effective preservative. Growing up in Colorado, I was accustomed to using salt to melt ice on sidewalks after a winter storm. I also have great memories of my father cranking an ice cream freezer, occasionally pouring salt on the ice to make it pack harder.

In all of my experiences with salt, I can only recall one use for salt that did not require dispersing the salt. My first car was a 1970 Mustang (worth more today than it was then). Back in the day before front-wheel drive vehicles, it had a very powerful engine and a very light rear end (the opposite of my body today). Consequently, it did not handle well on snow and ice, a common situation in Colorado. We always had fifty pound bags of salt in our basement that were used in the water softener. When winter arrived, my father would place four or five bags of salt in the trunk of my Mustang to increase the weight and improve the way it drove on slick roads. In that situation, the salt was just as valuable in the bag.

However, the way to get the most value out of salt is to utilize its ability to permeate the environment - out of the saltshaker.

Jesus identified His followers as the "salt of the earth" (Matthew 5:13). We are the ones who flavor and preserve the world. Without followers of Christ, the world becomes a tasteless, putrid place.

As I have already mentioned several times, one of the flaws that I see in the way we are doing church these days is that we might just be building bigger and better saltshakers. We have come to expect the church to be there for all of our needs. We understand the church to be the "go to" place for everything. It is our source of entertainment, recreation, fellowship, service, ministry, financial guidance, education, health services, sex education, counseling, family services, addiction recovery, and job searches. We even turn to the church when we want to find a good plumber or electrician. Parents want their children to be involved in church activities and recreational leagues because it is safer than other alternatives. Even adults play in a church softball league so they don't have to rub shoulders with other players who might enjoy a cold beer after the game.

Whenever you eat steak, do you ever dip each piece of meat in the saltshaker? Probably not! Instead, you sprinkle the salt on the meat - that is the way it works. Yet, when it comes to church, we expect those who need Christ to come immerse themselves in the church. It is like putting the meat in the salt. We have built our churches to be the place where people come in order to be flavored and preserved.

I don't know how many church softball leagues there are in my city, but what would happen if all of those who wanted to play in a church league simply sprinkled themselves in city and recreational leagues and lived out their witness. In other words, what if the salt got out of the saltshaker?

This problem is compounded because we are tempted to believe that we have fulfilled our role as salt when we show up at church on occasion. We might even feel especially "salty" if we invite a friend to come visit our saltshaker for a special Christmas show. It has become easy to define being a disciple of Jesus to mean little more than attending church. After all, what more do we need since all of our needs can be met at that place. Perhaps it is time to replace the image of the church as a saltshaker.

Sometimes when you go through the drive through and get a burger and fries, they put a couple of small paper packets of salt in the bottom of the sack. These packets contain just enough salt to add some taste to the potatoes or a little zest to the hamburger. All you do is rip open the small package, pour out the salt, and throw the packet away. The salt has served its purpose and made the meal tastier.

Those little paper packets are not designed to protect the salt or keep it from being used. They are temporary holders until the salt is needed. I wonder if there might be a lesson here for the way we do church. Perhaps it might be good to design our churches with the idea of making believers functional out there, in the world, rather than keeping them safe, away from the world. It would certainly free up a tremendous amount of resources if we stopped trying to build giant saltshakers.

There are some specific things we can do as the church to help us get out of the saltshaker and add flavor to the world. These are activities that point to Christ and contribute to the goal of keeping Him at the center.

One, often overlooked activity is the celebration of communion. Every celebration of communion is an experience of Christ with us (see 1 Corinthians 10:16). Describing communion, Leslie Newbigin said the church experiences a "foretaste of the reign of God in the midst of history." I grew up in a tradition that celebrated what we called, the Lord's Supper, once every three months. I think it was more a matter of physical convenience than theological conviction. Part of the rationale I frequently heard was that when it is done "too often" it can lose significance.

Now we celebrate communion every Sunday and the opposite is true. It has not lost, but actually gained significance for me. It is a basic New Testament principle that in order for a church to function properly, every member has a role to fulfill. I have several responsibilities at Bread Fellowship, not the least of which is to provide the bread for our weekly communion observance. During our short history we have tried several different approaches but it seems the one that works the best is for me to simply bring a small loaf of bread.

I am not unfamiliar with the workings of the Lord's Supper. When I was a very young child, after our church observed the Supper, my sister and I would finish off the juice and bread that was leftover. I'm sure we were allowed to do this because my mother has never thrown away anything in her life. We always considered it a treat to be able to recreate the event before being hustled off to bed on Sunday night. I will confess now that I always hoped for a small crowd at church since that meant more leftovers for us later.

Being the pastor of the same church for thirteen years, I have organized the Lord's Supper in every way imaginable to avoid falling into a meaningless routine. One of the most memorable times was provided by an unexpected source. We had a young mother, Rosalinda, who gave her life to Jesus one evening in her home. She and her children began attending church every week, always sitting on the front row. She was growing in her faith every Sunday.

The first Sunday that we observed the Supper was a new experience for her. As the Deacons took the bread trays and began to distribute the wafers, you could see Rosalinda, sitting on the front row, trying to figure out what to do. As the tray was extended to her, she did the only thing she knew to do. She placed her offering on the tray, on top of the bite sized wafers. From the front of the auditorium, I observed as people would snicker at the bread tray, containing some stale wafers and a couple of dollar bills that was passed around the room.

The event is nearly as memorable as the Gold Fish and chicken noodle soup fiasco in the early days of Bread Fellowship (a good story for another day). Perhaps the one thing that the Lord's Supper and weddings have in common is that in spite of the most meticulous planning, something will go wrong. At least at a wedding, someone is usually ready with a video camera to capture the event for YouTube.

At Bread Fellowship, when we finally settled on a routine where I am responsible for bringing the bread, Sharon and I developed our own routine. The only grocery store on our route to the church is the Super Mercado on Northside Drive. It is not the kind of place where we would normally shop but it has a fascination of its own. The grill is almost always cooking in the parking lot and the smell is very attractive. I plan to stop and get a few tacos on one of these trips. Few people inside the store, employees or customers, speak in English but it has never been a problem.

As you enter the store, one of the first items you come to is a large cabinet with a glass front door. Inside is a variety of breads, I suspect most of it is cooked fresh every morning. They sell a small loaf that is the ideal size for our little group at Bread Fellowship. The cost is three loaves for a dollar which means it only costs thirty-three and a third cents in order to remember the ultimate price paid by our Savior.

However, you must be careful in selecting the bread. They also sell a very similar looking loaf that is filled with jelly. Sharon ran into the store one Sunday evening and as we approached the church it hit her that she might have picked up the wrong loaf. Sure enough, when the bread was broken open for the Lord's Supper, we were surprised to see the grape jelly filling. I guess we could have completed the service without the juice since it was an all-in-one loaf. Fortunately, we had a small group that night so we all just pinched off the bread around the edges, without the jelly.

Being asked to bring the bread to Bread Fellowship is an honor. Even though we celebrate communion every week, the experience has always been meaningful to me. I leave with a new appreciation of Jesus' sacrifice and a strong attachment to the others in the room. It is my way of doing my part as the body of Christ. Sure, I have other responsibilities but this simple task is no less meaningful. Our worship is enhanced by something I do. You see, we are all necessary. Remember, contributing at Bread Fellowship may be as simple as stopping at the Mercado and getting a small loaf of bread.

The weekly celebration of communion is a powerful reminder of the reason we gather. It is all about Jesus.

Another activity that keeps us focused on Christ is ministry to the needy. Helping those in need was at the heart of Jesus' earthly work. The practice was continued by the early church as recorded in the Book of Acts. In fact, it is simply an expression of the concern of God for the poor that is expressed repeatedly throughout both the Old and New Testaments.

The Civil War provides a fascinating study for military historians. The Union forces of the North were much larger than the Confederate Army. In fact, there were more than one million Union soldiers compared to approximately 200,000 Confederate troops. However, one of the most serious weaknesses of the Union forces was a succession of Generals who were not aggressive enough to attack. They always waited for the enemy to begin the battles.

One of these early Generals was George B. McClellan. President Abraham Lincoln described McClellan as "a superb organizer. He has good points, but he won't fight." Later, he referred to his army as "the personal bodyguard of General McClellan."

Finally, in disgust, Lincoln wrote to General McClellan and said, "Would you please loan me this army if you don't intend to use it?"

This picture of the Union army reminds me of the church. The church has a massive army of powerful combatants but is losing ground to the enemy every day. In the past forty years, since Richard Nixon used the phrase, we have turned the "Silent Majority" into a strident minority. In many arenas, the church is considered an irrelevant relic in spite of the fact that many Christians are becoming louder and louder.

I believe the church has a large enough army to share the Gospel to all nations, feed the hungry, protect the unborn, and fulfill all the other tasks God has called us to do. But, there is a problem that is keeping all of these good things from happening.

If you will allow me to continue with the military theme, the problem begins with the fact that we are attempting to fight the wrong battle. It seems that many Christians are engaged in a conflict to protect a culture that no longer exists. Some are of the opinion that it was the culture of our nation's founding fathers that we must protect. Others, not wanting to return to the 18th century, are fighting for a culture from the middle of the 20th century, the "Father Knows Best" era.

The church is not to be about the business of defending any culture. Christianity can thrive in any environment. In fact, historically the church has probably done much better in the midst of hostile cultures than friendly cultures. While we have spent the past twenty or thirty years fighting for the culture, the center of Christianity appears to be moving to the Southern Hemisphere. We need to stop wasting our resources fighting a war that we have not been called to wage and get about the task of what God has called His church to do.

I also think that many Christians are fighting with the wrong motivation. They are at war in order to maintain their lifestyle. We all want freedom, a strong economy, the opportunity to get a good education, and the security of living in a place that is away from crime and immoral influences. However, as worthy as all of these goals might be, they are not the task of the church. The church has the higher calling of helping people find salvation that is far superior to anything culture can offer.

One of the reasons for the weakness of the church is that we want what everyone else wants. I listened to a friend recently lead a conference and he spoke about the difference in lifestyle between believers and non-believers. There is no difference, was his conclusion.

Our motivation for speaking out against sin is not so we can live in crime free neighborhoods but so sinners can be saved. Our motivation for getting involved in the health care debate is not so we can keep our taxes low but so we can help the poor have their illnesses treated. Our motivation to fix the economy is not so we can have a comfortable home in the suburbs but so the poorest of the poor can be lifted up. Our motivation for being on the frontlines of the abortion battle is not to identify those who are going to hell but to comfort those who are hurting. When sinners are saved, the poor are fed and lifted up, and the hurting are comforted, the attitude of the world toward the church will change radically.

Not only are we fighting the wrong battle with the wrong motivation, but we are also utilizing the wrong method. Our approach to the world can better be described as anger rather than love. We may not think we are angry but just expressing the judgment of God against sin. Sometimes my wife reminds me that I sound angry even though that was not my intent. If we are not careful, we can say good things in a way that communicates dislike.

The world has heard our anger, but they have not felt our love. When they are asked about Christians, they will use terms like angry, hateful, judgmental, and condescending. I grew up loving the church. The place was filled with people who loved me and took care of me. I had no doubts that the people of the church were flawed, but it did not matter because they always loved me.

I was contacted a few years ago on Facebook by an old friend from high school days. It has been at least thirty years since we had contact, but as soon as I saw Steve's name I was transported back to those great memories of church. We sang in the church choir together and we could drown out the rest of the choir with our great tenor voices. We both stood in the front row of the Billy Graham Crusade choir in Denver. One Sunday night Steve accidently dropped me down the stairs as we headed to the church basement for Bible study class. We spent countless hours together at church.

As a teenager, I knew there was nothing I could do nor any problem I could cause that would keep those church folks from loving me. I was never embarrassed to bring my friends to church because I knew they would be loved as well. Those who most need the church today will not turn to the church for fear of being judged or criticized.

The church is a powerful army with the potential of making a significant impact in the world. However, we are preoccupied with the wrong war, inspired by the wrong motivation, and employing the wrong method so we are in danger of being of little value to those who need the Gospel.

IS THE CHURCH ONLY FOR GOOD CHRISTIANS?

I recently read an article about an organization that provides background checks for churches. If a church wants to feel safe about those who volunteer to work with children or serve in a leadership position, it might be a good idea to get information about that person's past. The article was full of statistics and inferences, but it was not the numbers that caught my attention. It was the attitude of quoted interested parties that struck me as curious.

Researchers did what statisticians like to do. They took the numbers, applied them to a specific situation, and came to a conclusion. Don't worry if their conclusion is based on faulty logic and incomplete research. The researchers speculate that there are more than 60,000 people with some type of criminal history in Southern Baptist churches.

I am not sure why they chose to single out Southern Baptists. Do we really believe that Methodists are more law-abiding? I know some Southern Baptists who believe that "mixed bathing" is a walk on the wild side. For those of you younger than forty, "mixed bathing" does not refer to taking a shower with your girl friend. It means boys and girls swimming together, actually in the same body of water and wearing a complete swimsuit.

I am sure the background check folks were not searching for criminal backstrokers, or for the truly serious sinner who likes to spend Sunday afternoon at the mall. They identified people who had been accused and convicted of committing a felony, a significant crime.

"It is so important in this day and time to run these checks," said a church Secretary in Tennessee. "We just don't know who is coming into our church. We'd like to think everyone is a good Christian, but we can't know that."

I am concerned about the statement made by this church secretary. Apparently, one who has a criminal background cannot be a "good Christian." With that definition of a good Christian, we must eliminate a person like the Apostle Paul or anyone else who has experienced the amazing transforming power of salvation. If they would have kept records back in those days, Jesus Himself would have had a criminal record, condemned to capital punishment.

Jesus came to preach to the outcasts of society. Judgment will be on the basis of how faithful we were in visiting the prisoners. The reason the gospel is good news is because it offers release to the captive and salvation to the sinner.

Before you go off on a tangent and accuse me of missing the point that the purpose of these background checks is to protect our children from sexual abusers, let me assure you that I understand and agree that we must protect our children. However, my concern is that we become too comfortable with a church consisting only of people without blemishes. It is fine to have a few indiscretions, but if you should have a felony on your record, go somewhere else.

We have become a very judgmental society. Michael Vick, the football player involved in dog fighting, finished a two-year prison sentence that also cost him millions of dollars as a football player. He has served his time, appears to be remorseful, and wants to play football. Yet, there are many who want him banned from the game for life and do not want to be associated with him in any way.

Baseball player, Josh Hamilton has had a highly publicized struggle with drugs and alcohol that cost him three years of his life and also millions of dollars. He is winning the battle. However, he has had a couple of episodes where he messed up. He immediately confessed and apologized to his wife, his employer, and everyone else involved. Now that it has become public, people want him to be punished in some way.

A college basketball coach had an extra-marital fling six years ago but word got out. Consequently, a Baptist college where he was scheduled to address a leadership luncheon cancelled the appearance. The cancellation is in spite of the fact that he admitted his sin and apologized to his wife years ago.

I believe that the cruelty toward animals demonstrated by dog fighting is a terrible sin. I certainly think it is a sinful waste to throw away your life with drugs and alcohol. I am also a strong advocate of being faithful to your marriage. All of these men are sinners.

The place where sinners should feel the most love and acceptance might also be the place where they receive the greatest criticism – the church. I don't know about you, but when I go to church I want to "fit in." I want to belong, to be loved and accepted. The truth is the church should love me regardless of whether I fit it and in spite of my past and my appearance.

If I had the opportunity to talk to the church secretary who wants a church with only "good Christians," I guess I might remind her that the good Christians are in the church. However, those good Christians might also be the ones with the criminal history or at least the checkered past. It is not hypocritical for a fallen addict or sinning husband to belong to the church. If they do not feel welcome, it is because we have a great deal to learn about forgiveness.

It is time to tear down the fences we have erected to protect Jesus and ourselves. It is time to make all those who are sinners to be welcomed into the church. It is certainly time to put Christ at the center of our congregations and throw open the doors to anyone who wants to meet Him.

Even if you are just a casual Woody Allen fan, you are probably familiar with the movie, "Broadway Danny Rose." Danny Rose was a talent agent to a bunch of hopeful stars and a few who were well past their prime. He always went the extra mile for his clients, finding them jobs in out of the way places, tending to their personal needs and whims, and just being their best friend. He could always be counted on to do whatever they needed done. Danny's list of clients included a stuttering ventriloquist, a woman who made music on water-filled glasses, a piano playing bird act, a balloon folder, and a one legged tap dancer.

The movie ends with all of Danny's misfits gathered at his apartment for Thanksgiving dinner. They are eating frozen turkey dinners because it is cheaper and everyone is having a grand time. They don't ever say, but you get the feeling everyone who is there has no one else in their life, no where else to go on Thanksgiving. In a sense, this group of misfits has found a family and they have come together in Danny Rose's apartment to share a meal.

A couple of times during the movie, Danny referred to his Uncle Sidney's famous saying, "acceptance, forgiveness, and love." Those were the qualities that brought such a dispirited group of people to Danny Rose's apartment. They are also the qualities the church has to offer to the world. People really do not need a political agenda to follow, an economic philosophy to provide their needs, entertainment to fill their time, or empty promises to make their life happy. They need to be accepted, forgiven, and loved.

It is time to tear down the fences that keep this from happening.

Afterword

When I heard Glenn Hinson, who wrote the forward for this book, say thirty years ago in a seminary lecture, "God has a Center, but God has no circumference," a new imagination was planted within me. My entire lifetime of ministry has been an attempt to incarnate this Center in the love of Jesus Christ. Indeed, Christ is the Center.

I think I speak for most Christian ministers in saying that the substance of their work is the establishment of this center. But, the corollary to the establishment of this center is the disestablishment of the circumference, the boundary that the church constructs in order to preserve and sustain its institutional character. An institution always requires - frankly, demands - the assertion of control and the consolidation of power. The more and longer that control is asserted and that power is consolidated, the more distant this circumference gets from the original center it was designed to protect.

This construction/de-construction dynamic has been at work throughout the history of the church, and continues to shape the Christian churches today, including the one described at length in Terry Austin's lively book.

On the one hand, the location and establishment of Christ as the center of the community requires a construction. The construction of this center is accomplished with the Teachings of Jesus, (particularly the Sermon on the Mount and the parables), the declarative and charismatic energy of the Apostles after the resurrection (principally recorded in Acts), and the vision of an inclusive community of love implemented by Paul and later interpreted and outlined in his letters. Preaching, teaching, studying, and enacting these remarkable narratives will establish this creative Center of Christ. Just try it and see what happens.

But, on the other hand, the announcement of this vision and the telling of these stories and the implementation of this agenda always requires - no, again, demands - a concomitant disestablishment of the circumference that the institutional church has drawn in order to sustain and preserve itself. This circumference is made up of doctrines, offices, programs, buildings, procedures - in general, things that are not to be found in the apostolic, ancient writings listed above - and must be dismantled in order to make room for the construction of the center. But, as any honest institutional minister can attest, the dominant activity of the institutional churches focuses on the circumference, not the center. We pastors have been co-opted by and consumed with the managerial and administrative tasks of local church ministry, and are generally exhausted by it. As Terry pointedly observes, we were called to this work out of the center, and for the center, but it's the circumference that gets most of our attention.

It just isn't possible to establish the center and the circumference in equal measures of energy. One tends to displace the other. Any minister who has enthusiastically attempted the construction of a center will readily testify that work on that project has been as fulfilling as the de-construction of the circumference has been frustrating. The center of Christ and his love is simply too inclusive and imaginative to sustain much energy for the circumference, which pales in comparison. If you don't think this is true just ask somebody who does not go to church why he or she does not attend. They will not say it's because Jesus isn't interesting or compelling. Again, just try it and see what happens.

This tension between the center and the circumference in the life of the church is, of course, not new. It has marked the history of the Christian movement from the start, and can clearly be found in the letters of Paul. It characterized the break of the Way from the synagogue life in the first century, the occupation of all those pagan Greek temples by the worshiping community after Constantine (why else does every First Church have Corinthian columns?), the formation of the monastic order (somebody had to pray and make good wine), the protesting and reforming of the church in the 16th century, and the rise of denominationalism, particularly in America. All of this history is fraught with both spiritual failure and spiritual success, and whatever happens in your church will be also.

Now that you have read this book, ask yourself these questions: What am I protecting and preserving in my church? Where do I spend most of my time and energy in church? Who holds the congregational decision-making power and influence? What is their color? Gender? Economic class? Which of Jesus' parables challenges and touches me most? How is my church enacting those parables? What happened to Peter at Pentecost? What did he say? Is my church saying that? Living that? How we answer these questions determines how the establishment of the center is progressing in our faith communities.

For anyone who cares to observe it - and that includes most pastors and lay leaders (note Terry's analysis of that curious term) - we are definitely in a season when something old is passing away, giving rise to what Phyllis Tickle calls a "great emergence" of something new. For those of us who have a high ecclesiology - fancy language for a deep belief in the church as the Body of Christ - we believe that what is unfolding is less "new" than "renewed."

In this book, Terry Austin not only contributes to the growing conversation about why this building up and breaking down must be done in order for the promise of Christ to be fulfilled, but also gives practical pastoral counsel, drawing from a lifetime of church service, about how it is being done in one concrete community of Christ called Bread in Fort Worth, Texas. I have the pleasure of watching this pastor at work, and know he puts his money where his mouth is. It is of great benefit and enrichment to me to have Terry as a colleague and co-pastor at Bread. He is an engaging conversation partner and authentic shepherd, and I am fortunate to receive his great spirit.

Don't be afraid to try some of the things Terry describes here, and be sure not to take yourself too seriously. Do them with the self-deprecating humility and humor that Terry reveals here. There should be much "clowning" in Christian ministry, and when you have a colorful circle of misfits, seekers and refugees like Bread does, it isn't hard to laugh.

Charles Foster Johnson,
Co-Pastor, Bread Fellowship
Fort Worth, Texas

CPSIA information can be obtained at www.ICGtesting.com
Printed in the USA
LVOW091105150612

286250LV00001B/27/P